CHANGING COLORS

Work the last stitch to within one step of completion, hook new yarn *(Fig. 4)* and draw through all loops on hook.

Fig. 4

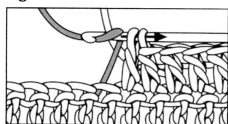

NO-SEW J

Hold Motifs with ʋ
or single crochet ir

Fig. 6

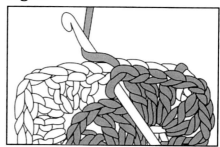

MW00807162

WHIPSTITCH

Hold two Blocks or Squares with **wrong** sides together. Beginning in corner stitch, sew through both pieces once to secure the beginning of the seam, leaving an ample yarn end to weave in later. Insert the needle from **front** to **back** through **both** loops on **both** pieces *(Fig. 5a)* or through **inside** loops of each stitch on **both** pieces *(Fig. 5b)*, ★ insert the needle from **front** to **back** through next stitch and pull yarn through; repeat from ★ across.

Fig. 5a

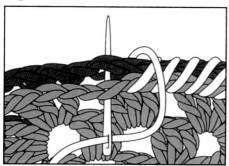

Fig. 5b

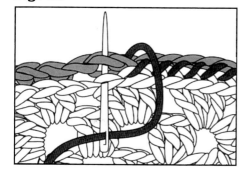

REVERSE SINGLE CROCHET

Working from **left** to **right**, insert hook in stitch to right of hook *(Fig. 7a)*, YO and draw through, under and to left of loop on hook (2 loops on hook) *(Fig. 7b)*, YO and draw through both loops on hook *(Fig. 7c)* **(reverse sc made, *Fig. 7d*)**.

Fig. 7a

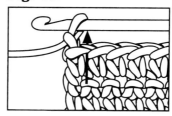

Fig. 7b

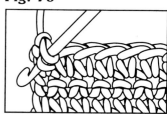

Fig. 7c

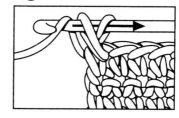

Fig. 7d

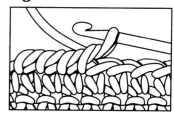

ALUMINUM CROCHET HOOKS													
U.S.	B-1	C-2	D-3	E-4	F-5	G-6	H-8	I-9	J-10	K-10½	N	P	Q
Metric - mm	2.25	2.75	3.25	3.50	3.75	4.00	5.00	5.50	6.00	6.50	9.00	10.00	15.00

Production Team: Writer - Susan Ackerman Carter; Technical Editor - Cathy Hardy; Editorial Writer - Suzie Puckett; Artist - John Rose; and Photo Stylists - Tiffany Huffman, Elizabeth Lackey, and Janna Laughlin.

Afghans made and instructions tested by Janet Akins, Connie Balogh, Belinda Baxter, Pam Bland, JoAnn Bowling, Mike Cates, Lee Ellis, Pat Funk, Katie Galucki, Kathleen Hardy, Vicki Kellogg, Patricia Little, Peggy Pierpaoli, Donna Soellner, Clare Stringer, Margaret Taverner, Carol Thompson, Mary Valen, and Cathy Wyatt.

First Prize

Rosalie DeVries

Rosalie DeVries of Arizona, our First-Prize winner, has been crocheting since she was a teenager. And for the past 23 years, she's been creating her own designs. "I wanted new and different patterns," she explains. Both Rosalie and her husband are now retired, so she enjoys spending her free time knitting, making woodcrafts, reading, traveling, baking, and most of all, crocheting! As the mother of two daughters, one stepdaughter, and one stepson, and the grandmother of six, Rosalie knows first-hand about the bond that forever links a mother and child. This symbolism was the inspiration for her lovely wrap of intertwining hearts.

HEART-TO-HEART

Finished Size: 43" x 47"

MATERIALS
Worsted Weight Yarn:
    White - 7½ ounces, (210 grams, 490 yards)
    Blue - 6 ounces, (170 grams, 395 yards)
    Lt Pink - 6 ounces, (170 grams, 395 yards)
    Pink - 5½ ounces, (160 grams, 360 yards)
Crochet hook, size G (4.00 mm) **or** size needed for gauge

GAUGE: Each Motif = 6¾"w x 9½"h

Gauge Swatch: 4"w x 3¾"h
Work same as First Heart.

STITCH GUIDE

DOUBLE TREBLE CROCHET
(abbreviated dtr)
YO 3 times, insert hook in sc indicated, YO and pull up a loop (5 loops on hook), (YO and draw through 2 loops on hook) 4 times.

SCALLOP
Ch 4, dc in fourth ch from hook.

LARGE SCALLOP
Ch 6, dc in sixth ch from hook.

FIRST MOTIF
FIRST HEART
FIRST LINK
With Blue, ch 16 **loosely**; being careful not to twist ch, join with slip st to form a ring.

Rnd 1 (Right side): Ch 3 **(counts as first dc, now and throughout)**, 5 dc in next ch, dc in next 5 chs, 5 dc in next ch, dc in next ch, 5 dc in next ch, dc in next 5 chs, place marker around last dc made to mark **right** side and st placement, 5 dc in last ch; join with slip st to first dc, finish off: 32 dc.

SECOND LINK
With same color as First Link, ch 16 **loosely**; being careful not to twist ch, insert end through middle of First Link from **back** to **front**, join with slip st to form a ring.

Rnd 1 (Right side): Ch 3, 5 dc in next ch, dc in next 5 chs, 4 dc in next ch, place marker around last dc made to mark **right** side and joining placement, dc in same st and in next ch, 5 dc in next ch, dc in next 5 chs, 5 dc in last ch; join with slip st to first dc, finish off: 32 dc.

Continued on page 5

TRIM

With **right** side of Second Link facing, join White with sc in same st as joining *(see Joining With Sc, page 1)*; sc in next dc, 2 sc in next dc, place marker in last sc made for joining placement, sc in same st and in next 2 dc, [insert hook in next dc, YO and pull up a loop, with **right** side of First Link facing, insert hook in marked dc, YO and pull up a loop, YO and draw through all 3 loops on hook **(counts as one sc)**], sc in next 2 dc, 2 sc in next dc, place marker in last sc made for joining placement, sc in same st and in next 11 dc; working through **both** thicknesses of **both** Links, sc in next dc **and** in marked dc on Second Link, sc in next 3 dc, 3 sc in next dc, sc in next 4 dc; working in dc on Second Link only, sc in last 9 dc; join with slip st to first sc, finish off: 44 sc.

SECOND HEART

Work First and Second Link same as First Heart.

TRIM

Joining Rnd: With **right** side of Second Link facing, join White with sc in same st as joining; sc in next 2 dc, with **right** side of **First Heart** facing and top edge toward you, drop loop from hook, insert hook from **front** to **back** in first marked sc, hook dropped loop and draw through, 2 sc in same st on **Second Heart**, sc in next 2 dc, [insert hook in next dc, YO and pull up a loop, with **right** side of First Link facing, insert hook in marked dc, YO and pull up a loop, YO and draw through all 3 loops on hook **(counts as one sc)**], sc in next 3 dc, drop loop from hook, insert hook from **front** to **back** in next marked sc on **First Heart**, hook dropped loop and draw through, 2 sc in same st on **Second Heart**, sc in next 11 dc; working through **both** thicknesses of **both** Links, sc in next dc **and** in marked dc on Second Link, sc in next 3 dc, 3 sc in next dc, sc in next 4 dc; working in dc on Second Link only, sc in last 9 dc; join with slip st to first sc, finish off: 44 sc.

BORDER

Rnd 1: With **right** side facing, join Pink with sc in center sc of 3-sc group at bottom point on either Heart; † work Scallop, skip next 2 sc, dc in next sc, work Scallop, skip next 2 sc, (dtr, work Large Scallop, dtr) in next sc, work Scallop, skip next 2 sc, dc in next sc, work Scallop, skip next 2 sc, sc in next sc, work Scallop, skip next 2 sc, dc in next sc, work Scallop, skip joining on next Heart and next 2 sc, dc in next sc, work Scallop, skip next 2 sc, sc in next sc, work Scallop, skip next 2 sc, dc in next sc, work Scallop, skip next 2 sc, (dtr, work Large Scallop, dtr) in next sc, work Scallop, skip next 2 sc, dc in next sc, work Scallop, skip next 2 sc †, sc in next sc, repeat from † to † once; join with slip st to first sc, finish off: 26 Scallops.

Rnd 2: With **right** side facing and working across short edge of Motif, join same color as Heart Links with slip st in ch-5 sp of first Large Scallop; ch 2 **(counts as first hdc)**, 8 hdc in same sp, ★ 5 hdc in ch-3 sp of each Scallop across to ch-5 sp of next Large Scallop, 9 hdc in ch-5 sp; repeat from ★ 2 times **more**, 5 hdc in ch-3 sp of each Scallop across; join with slip st to first hdc, finish off: 146 hdc.

Rnd 3: With **right** side facing and working across short edge of Motif, join White with sc in center hdc of first corner 9-hdc group; ch 5, sc in same st, † ch 3, skip next 2 hdc, sc in next hdc, ch 3, (sc in center hdc of next 5-hdc group, ch 3) 4 times, skip next 3 hdc, sc in next hdc, ch 3, skip next 2 hdc, (sc, ch 5, sc) in next hdc, ch 3, skip next 2 hdc, sc in next hdc, ch 3, (sc in center hdc of next 5-hdc group, ch 3) 7 times, skip next 3 hdc, sc in next hdc, ch 3, skip next 2 hdc †, (sc, ch 5, sc) in next hdc, repeat from † to † once; join with slip st to first sc, finish off: 38 sps.

ADDITIONAL MOTIFS

Note: The method used to connect the Motifs is a no-sew joining also known as "join-as-you-go". After the first Motif is made, each remaining Motif is worked through Rnd 2 of Border, then crocheted together as Rnd 3 is worked *(Fig. 6, page 2)*.

Using Blue or Light Pink for Heart Links, as indicated on Placement Diagram, page 6, work same as First Motif through Rnd 2 of Border: 146 hdc.

Rnd 3 (Joining rnd)**:** Work Side, End, or End and Side Joining as needed.

When joining corners, always work into the same ch as previous joining.

SIDE JOINING

Rnd 3 (Joining rnd)**:** With **right** side facing and working across short edge of Motif, join White with sc in center hdc of first corner 9-hdc group; † ch 3, skip next 2 hdc, sc in next hdc, ch 3, (sc in center hdc of next 5-hdc group, ch 3) 4 times, skip next 3 hdc, sc in next hdc, ch 3, skip next 2 hdc †, (sc, ch 5, sc) in next hdc, ch 3, skip next 2 hdc, sc in next hdc, ch 3, (sc in center hdc of next 5-hdc group, ch 3) 7 times, skip next 3 hdc, sc in next hdc, ch 3, skip next 2 hdc, (sc, ch 5, sc) in next hdc, repeat from † to † once, sc in next hdc, ch 2, holding Motifs with **wrong** sides together, sc in center ch of corresponding corner ch-5 on **previous Motif**, ch 2, sc in same st on **new Motif**, ch 1, sc in center ch of next ch-3 on **previous Motif**, ch 1, skip next 2 hdc on **new Motif**, sc in next hdc, ch 1, sc in center ch of next ch-3 on **previous Motif**, ch 1, (sc in center hdc of next 5-hdc group on **new Motif**, ch 1, sc in center ch of next ch-3 on **previous Motif**, ch 1) 7 times, skip next 3 hdc on **new Motif**, sc in next hdc, ch 1, sc in center ch of next ch-3 on **previous Motif**, ch 1, skip last 2 hdc on **new Motif**, sc in same st as first sc, ch 2, sc in center ch of next corner ch-5 on **previous Motif**, ch 2; join with slip st to first sc on **new Motif**, finish off.

END JOINING

Rnd 3 (Joining rnd): With **right** side facing and working across short edge of Motif, join White with sc in center hdc of first corner 9-hdc group; ch 5, sc in same st, ch 3, skip next 2 hdc, sc in next hdc, ch 3, (sc in center hdc of next 5-hdc group, ch 3) 4 times, skip next 3 hdc, sc in next hdc, ch 3, skip next 2 hdc, (sc, ch 5, sc) in next hdc, † ch 3, skip next 2 hdc, sc in next hdc, ch 3, (sc in center hdc of next 5-hdc group, ch 3) 7 times, skip next 3 hdc, sc in next hdc, ch 3, skip next 2 hdc †, sc in next hdc, ch 2, holding Motifs with **wrong** sides together, sc in center ch of corresponding corner ch-5 on **previous Motif**, ch 2, sc in same st on **new Motif**, ch 1, sc in center ch of next ch-3 on **previous Motif**, ch 1, skip next 2 hdc on **new Motif**, sc in next hdc, ch 1, sc in center ch of next ch-3 on **previous Motif**, ch 1, (sc in center hdc of next 5-hdc group on **new Motif**, ch 1, sc in center ch of next ch-3 on **previous Motif**, ch 1) 4 times, skip next 3 hdc on **new Motif**, sc in next hdc, ch 1, sc in center ch of next ch-3 on **previous Motif**, ch 1, skip next 2 hdc on **new Motif**, sc in next hdc, ch 2, sc in center ch of next corner ch-5 on **previous Motif**, ch 2, sc in same st on **new Motif**, repeat from † to † once; join with slip st to first sc, finish off.

END AND SIDE JOINING

Rnd 3 (Joining rnd): With **right** side facing and working across short edge of Motif, join White with sc in center hdc of first corner 9-hdc group; ch 3, skip next 2 hdc, sc in next hdc, ch 3, (sc in center hdc of next 5-hdc group, ch 3) 4 times, skip next 3 hdc, sc in next hdc, ch 3, skip next 2 hdc, (sc, ch 5, sc) in next hdc, ch 3, skip next 2 hdc, sc in next hdc, ch 3, (sc in center hdc of next 5-hdc group, ch 3) 7 times, skip next 3 hdc, sc in next hdc, ch 3, skip next 2 hdc, sc in next hdc, ch 2, holding Motifs with **wrong** sides together, sc in center ch of corresponding corner ch-5 on **previous Motif**, ch 2, sc in same st on **new Motif**, ch 1, sc in center ch of next ch-3 on **previous Motif**, ch 1, skip next 2 hdc on **new Motif**, sc in next hdc, ch 1, sc in center ch of next ch-3 on **previous Motif**, ch 1, (sc in center hdc of next 5-hdc group on **new Motif**, ch 1, sc in center ch of next ch-3 on **previous Motif**, ch 1) 4 times, skip next 3 hdc on **new Motif**, sc in next hdc, ch 1, sc in center ch of next ch-3 on **previous Motif**, ch 1, skip next 2 hdc on **new Motif**, sc in next hdc, ch 2, sc in center ch of next corner ch-5 on **previous Motif**, ch 2, sc in same st on **new Motif**, ch 1, sc in center ch of next ch-3 on **previous Motif**, ch 1, skip next 2 hdc on **new Motif**, sc in next hdc, ch 1, sc in center ch of next ch-3 on **previous Motif**, ch 1, (sc in center hdc of next 5-hdc group on **new Motif**, ch 1, sc in center ch of next ch-3 on **previous Motif**, ch 1) 7 times, skip next 3 hdc on **new Motif**, sc in next hdc, ch 1, sc in center ch of next ch-3 on **previous Motif**, ch 1, skip last 2 hdc on **new Motif**, sc in same st as first sc, ch 2, sc in center ch of next corner ch-5 on **previous Motif**, ch 2; join with slip st to first sc on **new Motif**, finish off.

EDGING

Rnd 1: With **right** side facing, join Pink with sc in center ch of any corner ch-5; work Scallop, sc in same st as last sc made, work Scallop, ★ † [(sc in center ch of next ch-3, work Scallop) across to next joining, sc in joining, work Scallop] across to last Motif, (sc in center ch of next ch-3, work Scallop) across to next corner ch-5 †, (sc, work Scallop) twice in center ch of corner ch-5; repeat from ★ 2 times **more**, then repeat from † to † once; join with slip st to first sc, finish off.

Rnd 2: With **right** side facing and working in center ch of ch-3 on Scallops, join White with sc in any corner Scallop; ch 1, sc in same st, ch 3, (sc in next Scallop, ch 3) across to next corner Scallop, ★ (sc, ch 1, sc) in corner Scallop, ch 3, (sc in next Scallop, ch 3) across to next corner Scallop; repeat from ★ 2 times **more**; join with slip st to first sc, finish off.

Rnd 3: With **right** side facing, join Blue with sc in any corner ch; work Scallop, sc in same st as last sc made, work Scallop, (sc in center ch of next ch-3, work Scallop) across to next corner ch, ★ (sc, work Scallop) twice in corner ch, (sc in center ch of next ch-3, work Scallop) across to next corner ch; repeat from ★ 2 times **more**; join with slip st to first sc, finish off.

Rnd 4: Repeat Rnd 2.

Rnd 5: With Lt Pink, repeat Rnd 3.

Rnd 6: Repeat Rnd 2.

Rnd 7: With Pink, repeat Rnd 3.

Rnd 8: Repeat Rnd 2; do **not** finish off.

Rnd 9: Ch 1, sc in same st, ch 1, skip next corner ch, sc in next sc, ch 1, ★ (sc in center ch of next ch-3, ch 1, sc in next sc, ch 1) across to next corner ch, skip corner ch, sc in next sc, ch 1; repeat from ★ 2 times **more**, sc in center ch of next ch-3, ch 1, (sc in next sc, ch 1, sc in center ch of next ch-3, ch 1) across; join with slip st to first sc.

Rnd 10: Ch 1, working from **left** to **right**, work reverse sc in next sc (*Figs. 7a-d, page 2*), ch 1, (work reverse sc in next sc, ch 1) around; join with slip st to first st, finish off.

PLACEMENT DIAGRAM

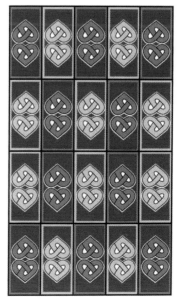

6

Second Prize

Leana Moon

Leana Moon of Texas, our Second-Prize winner, was hooked on crochet by the age of 17. "A friend showed me the basic stitches. I went right out and bought a 'Learn to Crochet' booklet, and I haven't stopped since," she says. Leana and her husband, Jack, are both retired and enjoy gardening and traveling when they have the opportunity. She loves crocheting afghans, slippers, sweaters, and vests for her children, grandchildren, and great-grandchildren. She came up with her colorful patchwork design to use up some of the yarn scraps she had left over from the many baby outfits she had crocheted.

KALEIDOSCOPE

Finished Size: 36" x 46½"

MATERIALS
Worsted Weight Yarn:
   White - 11 ounces, (310 grams, 620 yards)
   Scraps - 19½ ounces,
      (550 grams, 1,100 yards) **total**
         Note: We used 8 different colors.
Crochet hook, size H (5.00 mm) **or** size needed
   for gauge
Yarn needle

GAUGE: Each Square = 10½"

Gauge Swatch: 3" square
Work same as Square Center through Rnd 2.

STITCH GUIDE

BEGINNING DECREASE
Pull up a loop in first 2 sc, YO and draw through all 3 loops on hook **(counts as one sc)**.

DECREASE
Pull up a loop in next 2 sc, YO and draw through all 3 loops on hook **(counts as one sc)**.

SQUARE (Make 12)
CENTER
With Scrap color desired, ch 4; join with slip st to form a ring.

Rnd 1 (Right side)**:** Ch 3 **(counts as first dc, now and throughout)**, 2 dc in ring, (ch 3, 3 dc in ring) 3 times, ch 1, hdc in first dc to form last ch-3 sp: 12 dc and 4 ch-3 sps.

Note: Loop a short piece of yarn around any stitch to mark Rnd 1 as **right** side.

Rnd 2: Ch 3, 2 dc in last ch-3 sp made, ch 1, ★ (3 dc, ch 3, 3 dc) in next ch-3 sp, ch 1; repeat from ★ 2 times **more**, 3 dc in same sp as first dc, ch 1, hdc in first dc to form last ch-3 sp: 24 dc and 8 sps.

Rnd 3: Ch 3, 2 dc in last ch-3 sp made, ch 1, 3 dc in next ch-1 sp, ch 1, ★ (3 dc, ch 3, 3 dc) in next ch-3 sp, ch 1, 3 dc in next ch-1 sp, ch 1; repeat from ★ 2 times **more**, 3 dc in same sp as first dc, ch 3; join with slip st to first dc, finish off: 36 dc and 12 sps.

Continued on page 54.

Third Prize

Sandra L. Rideout

Sandy Rideout of Kentucky, our Third-Prize winner, is a crafter of "all kinds of things." In addition to crochet, which she has done "on and off" for 25 years, she also knits, sews, and quilts. Designing her own patterns, however, is something she's only been doing for about 7 years. A pastor's wife, homemaker, and mother, Sandy likes crocheting a variety of projects, both small and large. She even crocheted a room-size rug once. "I called it my therapy!" she laughs. Sandy's idea for making a blanket covered with sweet little gingerboys was triggered by the warm comfort children get from the aroma of fresh-baked goodies.

GINGER BABIES

Finished Size: 40½" x 46½"

MATERIALS
Worsted Weight Yarn:
    Ecru - 20½ ounces, (580 grams, 1,345 yards)
    Rose - 6½ ounces, (180 grams, 425 yards)
    Tan - 5 ounces, (140 grams, 330 yards)
    Brown - small amount
Crochet hooks, sizes F (3.75 mm), H (5.00 mm), **and** K (6.50 mm) **or** sizes needed for gauge
Yarn needle

GAUGE: Each Block = 10½"w x 12½"h
              Each Square = 2¼"

Gauge Swatch: 3" square
With Ecru and using largest size hook, ch 10 **loosely**.
Rows 1-8: Work same as Block Center: 9 sts.
Finish off.

STITCH GUIDE

BEGINNING DECREASE
Pull up a loop in first 2 sc, YO and draw through all 3 loops on hook **(counts as one sc)**.

DECREASE
Pull up a loop in next 2 sc, YO and draw through all 3 loops on hook **(counts as one sc)**.

BLOCK (Make 9)
CENTER
With Ecru and using largest size hook, ch 28 **loosely**.

Row 1: Sc in second ch from hook, (dc in next ch, sc in next ch) across: 27 sts.

Row 2 (Right side)**:** Ch 3 **(counts as first dc, now and throughout)**, turn; (sc in next dc, dc in next sc) across.

Note: Loop a short piece of yarn around any stitch to mark Row 2 as **right** side and bottom edge.

Row 3: Ch 1, turn; sc in first dc, (dc in next sc, sc in next dc) across.

Row 4: Ch 3, turn; (sc in next dc, dc in next sc) across.

Rows 5-29: Repeat Rows 3 and 4, 12 times; then repeat Row 3 once **more**; at end of Row 29, do **not** finish off.

Continued on page 11.

BORDER

Rnd 1: Ch 3, turn; (sc, dc) in first sc, sc in next dc, (dc in next sc, sc in next dc) across to last sc, (dc, sc, dc) in last sc; working in end of rows, sc in same row, (dc in next row, sc in next row) across; working in free loops of beginning ch *(Fig. 3, page 1)*, (dc, sc, dc) in ch at base of first sc, sc in next ch, (dc in next ch, sc in next ch) across to last ch, (dc, sc, dc) in last ch; working in end of rows, sc in same row, (dc in next row, sc in next row) across; join with slip st to first dc, finish off: 120 sts.

Rnd 2: With **right** side facing and using largest size hook, join Rose with dc in first sc **after** joining *(see Joining With Dc, page 1)*; (sc, dc) in same st, sc in next dc, ★ (dc in next sc, sc in next dc) across to center sc of next corner 3-st group, (dc, sc, dc) in center sc, sc in next dc; repeat from ★ 2 times **more**, (dc in next sc, sc in next dc) across; join with slip st to first dc, finish off: 128 sts.

SHORT STRIP (Make 12)

With Ecru and using largest size hook, ch 30 **loosely**, place marker in fourth ch from hook for st placement.

Foundation Row (Right side): Dc in back ridge of sixth ch from hook *(Fig. 1, page 1)*, ★ ch 1, skip next ch, dc in back ridge of next ch; repeat from ★ across: 13 dc and 13 sps.

Note: Mark Foundation Row as **right** side.

Rnd 1: Ch 6 **(counts as first dc plus ch 3)**, do **not** turn; dc in top of last dc made on Foundation Row, ch 3; working in free loops of beginning ch, (dc, ch 3, dc) in first ch, ch 1, skip next ch, ★ dc in next ch, ch 1, skip next ch; repeat from ★ across to marked ch, (dc, ch 3) twice in marked ch, skip next ch, (dc, ch 3, dc) in next ch, ch 1, (dc in next dc, ch 1) across; join with slip st to first dc, finish off.

LONG STRIP (Make 12)

With Ecru and using largest size hook, ch 34 **loosely**, place marker in fourth ch from hook for st placement.

Foundation Row (Right side): Dc in back ridge of sixth ch from hook, ★ ch 1, skip next ch, dc in back ridge of next ch; repeat from ★ across: 15 dc and 15 sps.

Note: Mark Foundation Row as **right** side.

Rnd 1: Ch 6 **(counts as first dc plus ch 3)**, do **not** turn; dc in top of last dc made on Foundation Row, ch 3; working in free loops of beginning ch, (dc, ch 3, dc) in first ch, ch 1, skip next ch, ★ dc in next ch, ch 1, skip next ch; repeat from ★ across to marked ch, (dc, ch 3) twice in marked ch, skip next ch, (dc, ch 3, dc) in next ch, ch 1, (dc in next dc, ch 1) across; join with slip st to first dc, finish off.

SQUARE (Make 16)

With Ecru and using medium size hook, ch 5; join with slip st to form a ring.

Rnd 1 (Right side): Ch 3, 2 dc in ring, ch 2, (3 dc in ring, ch 2) 3 times; join with slip st to first dc, finish off: 12 dc and 4 ch-2 sps.

Note: Mark Rnd 1 as **right** side.

Rnd 2: With **right** side facing and using medium size hook, join Rose with dc in any ch-2 sp; (2 dc, ch 2, 3 dc) in same sp, ch 1, ★ (3 dc, ch 2, 3 dc) in next ch-2 sp, ch 1; repeat from ★ 2 times **more**; join with slip st to first dc, finish off: 24 dc and 8 sps.

GINGERBREAD MAN (Make 9)
HEAD

With Tan and using medium size hook, ch 8 **loosely**.

Row 1: Sc in second ch from hook and in next 6 chs: 7 sc.

Row 2 (Right side): Ch 1, turn; 2 sc in first sc, sc in next 5 sc, 2 sc in last sc: 9 sc.

Note: Mark Row 2 as **right** side.

Row 3: Ch 1, turn; sc in each sc across.

Row 4: Ch 1, turn; 2 sc in first sc, sc in next 7 sc, 2 sc in last sc: 11 sc.

Rows 5-7: Ch 1, turn; sc in each sc across.

Row 8: Ch 1, turn; work beginning decrease, sc in next 7 sc, decrease: 9 sc.

Row 9: Ch 1, turn; work beginning decrease, sc in next 5 sc, decrease; do **not** finish off: 7 sc.

ARMS AND BODY

Row 1: Ch 7 **loosely**, turn; sc in second ch from hook and in next 5 chs, sc in last 7 sc: 13 sc.

Row 2: Ch 7 **loosely**, turn; sc in second ch from hook and in next 5 chs, sc in next 12 sc, 2 sc in last sc: 20 sc.

Row 3: Ch 1, turn; 2 sc in first sc, sc in next 18 sc, 2 sc in last sc: 22 sc.

Row 4: Ch 1, turn; 2 sc in first sc, sc in next sc and in each sc across: 23 sc.

Row 5: Ch 1, turn; sc in each sc across.

Row 6: Ch 1, turn; sc in each sc across to last 2 sc, decrease: 22 sc.

Row 7: Ch 1, turn; work beginning decrease, sc in next 18 sc, decrease: 20 sc.

Row 8: Ch 1, turn; work beginning decrease, sc in next 15 sc, leave remaining 3 sc unworked: 16 sc.

Row 9: Ch 1, turn; sc in first 13 sc, leave remaining 3 sc unworked: 13 sc.

Row 10: Ch 1, turn; 2 sc in first sc, sc in next 11 sc, 2 sc in last sc: 15 sc.

Rows 11 and 12: Ch 1, turn; sc in each sc across.

Row 13: Ch 1, turn; 2 sc in first sc, sc in next 13 sc, 2 sc in last sc: 17 sc.

Rows 14-18: Ch 1, turn; sc in each sc across; at end of Row 18, do **not** finish off.

FIRST LEG

Row 1: Ch 1, turn; sc in first 8 sc, leave remaining 9 sc unworked: 8 sc.

Rows 2-5: Ch 1, turn; sc in each sc across.

Row 6: Ch 1, turn; work beginning decrease, sc in next 4 sc, decrease: 6 sc.

Row 7: Ch 1, turn; work beginning decrease, sc in next 2 sc, decrease: 4 sc.

Row 8: Ch 1, turn; work beginning decrease, decrease; finish off: 2 sc.

SECOND LEG

Row 1: With **right** side facing and using medium size hook, skip one sc from First Leg and join Tan with sc in next sc on Row 18 of Body *(see Joining With Sc, page 1)*; sc in last 7 sc: 8 sc.

Rows 2-5: Ch 1, turn; sc in each sc across.

Row 6: Ch 1, turn; work beginning decrease, sc in next 4 sc, decrease: 6 sc.

Row 7: Ch 1, turn; work beginning decrease, sc in next 2 sc, decrease: 4 sc.

Row 8: Ch 1, turn; work beginning decrease, decrease; do **not** finish off: 2 sc.

TRIM

Rnd 1: Ch 1, turn; sc evenly around increasing or decreasing as necessary to keep Gingerbread Man laying flat; join with slip st to first sc, finish off.

Rnd 2: With **right** side facing and using medium size hook, join Rose with slip st in any sc; ch 1, (slip st in next sc, ch 1) around; join with slip st to joining slip st, finish off.

BOW

With Rose, using smallest size hook, and leaving a long end for sewing, ch 18, slip st in tenth ch from hook, ch 10, slip st in same st, ch 8; finish off.

Thread yarn needle with a double strand of Brown. Using photo as a guide, add a French knot for each eye and for 3 buttons as follows:

Bring needle up at 1. Wrap yarn around needle once and insert at 2, holding end of yarn with non-stitching fingers *(Fig. 8)*. Tighten knot; then pull needle through, holding yarn until it must be released.

Fig. 8

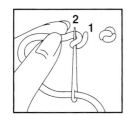

With long end and using photo as a guide for placement, tack Bow to Gingerbread Man.
Using Placement Diagram as a guide, sew a Gingerbread Man to center of each Block.

ASSEMBLY

With Ecru, using Placement Diagram as a guide, and working through **both** loops, whipstitch pieces together as follows *(Fig. 5a, page 2)*:
Form 4 vertical strips of 4 Squares and 3 Long Strips each, beginning in second ch of corner ch-2 on Square and in center ch of corner ch-3 on Strip, and ending in first ch of next corner ch-2 on Square and in center ch of next corner ch-3 on Strip.
Then form 3 vertical strips of 4 Short Strips and 3 Blocks each, beginning and ending in corner sc on Block and center ch of corner ch-3 on Strip.
Whipstitch strips together in same manner.

PLACEMENT DIAGRAM

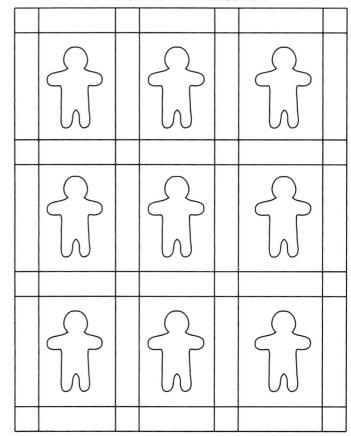

EDGING

Rnd 1: With **right** side facing and using largest size hook, join Rose with dc in any corner ch-2 sp; (sc, dc) in same sp, ★ † [(skip next dc, sc in next dc, dc in next sp) twice, sc in next joining, dc in next sp, (sc in next dc, dc in next sp) across to next joining, sc in next joining, dc in next sp] 3 times, skip next dc, sc in next dc, dc in next sp, skip next dc, sc in next dc †, (dc, sc, dc) in next corner ch-2 sp; repeat from ★ 2 times **more**, then repeat from † to † once; join with slip st to first dc: 480 sts.

Rnd 2: Ch 1, working from **left** to **right**, work reverse sc in each st around *(Figs. 7a-d, page 2)*; join with slip st to first st, finish off.

LAVENDER LACE

Finished Size: 37½" x 47"

MATERIALS
Worsted Weight Yarn:
   20 ounces, (570 grams, 1,310 yards)
Crochet hook, size H (5.00 mm) **or** size needed
   for gauge
⅜"w Ribbon - 4¼ yards
Sewing needle and thread

GAUGE: In pattern, 3 repeats = 4¾";
             8 rows = 4½"

Gauge Swatch: 6"w x 5"h
Ch 24 **loosely**.
Work same as Afghan Body for 9 rows.
Finish off.

AFGHAN BODY
Ch 120 **loosely**, place marker in third ch from hook for
st placement.

Row 1 (Right side)**:** Sc in back ridge of second ch from
hook **(Fig. 1, page 1)** and each ch across: 119 sc.

Note: Loop a short piece of yarn around any stitch to
mark Row 1 as **right** side.

Row 2: Ch 3 **(counts as first dc, now and
throughout)**, turn; dc in next 2 sc, skip next 2 sc, (2 dc,
ch 2, 2 dc) in next sc, ★ skip next 2 sc, dc in next sc, skip
next 2 sc, (2 dc, ch 2, 2 dc) in next sc; repeat from ★
across to last 5 sc, skip next 2 sc, dc in last 3 sc: 100 dc
and 19 ch-2 sps.

Row 3: Ch 3, turn; dc in next dc, (2 dc, ch 2, 2 dc) in
next dc, ★ dc in next ch-2 sp, skip next 2 dc, (2 dc, ch 2,
2 dc) in next dc; repeat from ★ across to last 2 dc, dc in
last 2 dc: 103 dc and 20 ch-2 sps.

Row 4: Ch 3, turn; dc in next dc and in next ch-2 sp,
★ skip next 2 dc, (2 dc, ch 2, 2 dc) in next dc, skip next
2 dc, dc in next ch-2 sp; repeat from ★ across to last
4 dc, skip next 2 dc, dc in last 2 dc: 100 dc and
19 ch-2 sps.

Rows 5-74: Repeat Rows 3 and 4, 35 times; at end of
Row 74, do **not** finish off.

EDGING
Rnd 1 (Eyelet rnd)**:** Ch 5 **(counts as first dc plus
ch 2)**, turn; skip next dc, dc in next dc, ch 2, ★ dc in
next ch-2 sp, ch 2, skip next 2 dc, dc in next dc, ch 2;
repeat from ★ across to last 2 dc, skip next dc, (dc, ch 3,
dc) in last dc, ch 2; working in end of rows, dc in first
row, ch 2, (dc in next row, ch 2) across to last sc row,
skip last sc row; working in free loops of beginning ch
(Fig. 3, page 1), (dc, ch 3, dc) in first ch, ch 2, skip next
ch, dc in next ch, ch 2, (skip next 2 chs, dc in next ch,
ch 2) across to marked ch, skip marked ch, (dc, ch 3, dc)
in next ch, ch 2; working in end of rows, skip first sc row
(dc in next row, ch 2) across, dc in same st as first dc,
ch 2, sc in first dc to form last ch-3 sp: 232 sps.

Rnd 2: Ch 3, dc in last ch-3 sp made, ✝ 3 dc in next
ch-2 sp, 2 dc in next ch-2 sp and in each ch-2 sp across
to within one ch-2 sp of next corner ch-3 sp, 3 dc in next
ch-2 sp, (2 dc, ch 3, 2 dc) in corner ch-3 sp ✝, 2 dc in
each ch-2 sp across to next corner ch-3 sp, (2 dc, ch 3,
2 dc) in corner ch-3 sp, repeat from ✝ to ✝ once, 2 dc in
each ch-2 sp across and in same sp as first dc, ch 2, sc in
first dc to form last ch-3 sp: 476 dc and 4 ch-3 sps.

Rnd 3: Ch 1, sc in last ch-3 sp made, ch 4, skip next
2 dc, (sc in next dc, ch 4, skip next 2 dc) across to next
corner ch-3 sp, ★ (sc, ch 4) twice in corner ch-3 sp, skip
next 2 dc, (sc in next dc, ch 4, skip next 2 dc) across to
next corner ch-3 sp; repeat from ★ 2 times **more**, sc in
same sp as first sc, ch 3, sc in first sc to form last ch-4 sp
164 ch-4 sps.

Rnds 4-7: Ch 1, sc in last ch-4 sp made, ch 4, (sc in
next ch-4 sp, ch 4) across to next corner ch-4 sp, ★ (sc,
ch 4) twice in corner ch-4 sp, (sc in next ch-4 sp, ch 4)
across to next corner ch-4 sp; repeat from ★ 2 times
more, sc in same sp as first sc, ch 3, sc in first sc to form
last ch-4 sp.

Rnd 8: Ch 1, sc in last ch-4 sp made, ch 4, (sc in next
ch-4 sp, ch 4) across to next corner ch-4 sp, ★ (sc,
ch 4) 3 times in corner ch-4 sp, (sc in next ch-4 sp, ch 4)
across to next corner ch-4 sp; repeat from ★ 2 times
more, (sc, ch 4) twice in same sp as first sc; join with
slip st to first sc, finish off.

Using photo as a guide, weave ribbon through Eyelet rnd
and tack ends to wrong side.

Design by Leana Moon.

MOTHER'S LOVE

Finished Size: 38" x 47½"

MATERIALS
Worsted Weight Yarn:
    28 ounces, (800 grams, 1,580 yards)
Crochet hook, size H (5.00 mm) **or** size needed
    for gauge
⅜" Ribbon - 5 yards
Sewing needle and thread

GAUGE: In pattern, (7 dc, ch 1) twice = 4¾";
           6 rows = 3¾"

Gauge Swatch: 6¼"w x 4½"h
Ch 23 **loosely**.
Work same as Afghan Body for 7 rows.
Finish off.

STITCH GUIDE

PUFF ST
YO, insert hook in dc indicated, YO and pull up a loop even with loop on hook, (YO, insert hook in **same** st, YO and pull up a loop even with loop on hook) 3 times (9 loops on hook), YO and draw through 8 loops on hook, YO and draw through both loops on hook.

LOOP STITCH *(abbreviated Loop St)*
Insert hook in st indicated, wrap yarn around index finger of left hand 2 times **more**, insert hook through all 3 strands on finger following direction indicated by arrow *(Fig. 9a)*, being careful to hook all strands *(Fig. 9b)*, draw through st pulling both loops to measure approximately 1", remove finger from loops, YO and draw through all 4 loops on hook **(Loop St made, Fig. 9c)**.

Fig. 9a

Fig. 9b

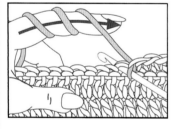
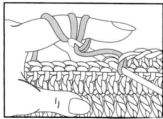

Fig. 9c

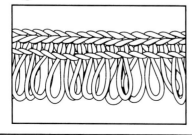

AFGHAN BODY
Ch 119 **loosely**, place marker in third ch from hook for st placement.

Row 1 (Right side)**:** Dc in fourth ch from hook **(3 skipped chs count as first dc)**, ch 1, ★ skip next ch, dc in next 7 chs, ch 1; repeat from ★ across to last 3 chs, skip next ch, dc in last 2 chs: 102 dc and 15 ch-1 sps.

Note: Loop a short piece of yarn around any stitch to mark Row 1 as **right** side.

Row 2: Ch 3 **(counts as first dc, now and throughout)**, turn; dc in next dc, ch 1, dc in next 2 dc, ch 1, skip next dc, work Puff St in next dc, ch 1, ★ skip next dc, (dc in next 2 dc, ch 1) twice, skip next dc, work Puff St in next dc, ch 1; repeat from ★ across to last 5 dc skip next dc, dc in next 2 dc, ch 1, dc in last 2 dc: 60 dc, 14 Puff Sts, and 43 ch-1 sps.

Row 3: Ch 3, turn; dc in next dc, ch 1, dc in next 2 dc, ★ dc in next ch-1 sp and in next Puff St, dc in next ch-1 sp and in next 2 dc, ch 1, dc in next 2 dc; repeat from ★ across: 102 dc and 15 ch-1 sps.

Row 4: Ch 3, turn; dc in next dc, ch 1, ★ dc in next dc, ch 1, (skip next dc, dc in next dc, ch 1) 3 times; repeat from ★ across to last 2 dc, dc in last 2 dc: 60 dc and 57 ch-1 sps.

Row 5: Ch 3, turn; dc in next dc, ch 1, ★ dc in next dc, (dc in next ch-1 sp and in next dc) 3 times, ch 1; repeat from ★ across to last 2 dc, dc in last 2 dc: 102 dc and 15 ch-1 sps.

Repeat Rows 2-5 for pattern until Afghan Body measures approximately 44½" from beginning ch, ending by working Row 3; do **not** finish off.

EDGING
Rnd 1 (Eyelet rnd)**:** Ch 3, turn; (dc, ch 2, 2 dc) in same st, dc in next dc, ch 1, dc in next dc, ★ ch 1, (skip next dc, dc in next dc, ch 1) 3 times, dc in next dc; repeat from ★ across to last dc, (2 dc, ch 2, 2 dc) in last dc, ch 1; working across end of rows, (dc in top of next row, ch 1) across; (2 dc, ch 2, 2 dc) in marked ch, working in free loops of beginning ch *(Fig. 3, page 1)*, dc in next ch, (ch 1, skip next ch, dc in next ch) across to last ch, (2 dc, ch 2, 2 dc) in last ch, ch 1; working across end of rows, (dc in top of next row, ch 1) across; join with slip st to first dc.

Rnd 2: Ch 1, do **not** turn; sc in same st and in each dc and each ch-1 sp around working 3 sc in each corner ch-2 sp; join with slip st to first sc.

Rnds 3-5: Ch 1, work Loop St in same st and in each st around working 3 Loop Sts in center st of each corner 3-st group; join with slip st to first st.

Finish off.

Using photo as a guide, weave ribbon through Eyelet rnd and tack ends to wrong side.

15 *Design by Joyce L. Rodriguez.*

BUNNY HUG

Finished Size: 36" x 46½"

MATERIALS
Worsted Weight Yarn:
  32 ounces, (910 grams, 1,810 yards)
Crochet hook, size H (5.00 mm) **or** size needed
  for gauge

GAUGE: In pattern, (Popcorn, 7 tr) twice = 4½";
  6 rows = 4¼"

Gauge Swatch: 5¾"w x 3¼"h
Ch 21 **loosely**.
Work same as Afghan Body for 4 rows.
Finish off.

STITCH GUIDE

> **TREBLE CROCHET** *(abbreviated tr)*
> YO twice, insert hook in st indicated, YO and pull up
> a loop (4 loops on hook), (YO and draw through
> 2 loops on hook) 3 times.
>
> **POPCORN**
> 5 Dc in st indicated, drop loop from hook, insert
> hook in first dc of 5-dc group, hook dropped loop
> and draw through, ch 1 to close.

AFGHAN BODY
Ch 117 **loosely**, place marker in third ch from hook for
st placement.

Row 1 (Right side): Work Popcorn in fourth ch from
hook, ★ skip next 3 chs, 7 tr in next ch, skip next 3 chs,
work Popcorn in next ch; repeat from ★ across to last ch,
dc in last ch: 15 Popcorns and 14 7-tr groups.

Note: Loop a short piece of yarn around any stitch to
mark Row 1 as **right** side.

Row 2: Ch 3 **(counts as first dc, now and
throughout)**, turn; ★ dc in closing ch of next Popcorn,
skip next 3 tr, 7 tr in next tr, skip next 3 tr; repeat from ★
across to last Popcorn, dc in closing ch of last Popcorn
and in next ch: 17 dc and 14 7-tr groups.

Row 3: Ch 3, turn; work Popcorn in next dc, ★ skip
next 3 tr, 7 tr in next tr, skip next 3 tr, work Popcorn in
next dc; repeat from ★ across to last dc, dc in last dc:
15 Popcorns and 14 7-tr groups.

Row 4: Ch 3, turn; dc in closing ch of next Popcorn,
★ skip next 3 tr, 7 tr in next tr, skip next 3 tr, dc in
closing ch of next Popcorn; repeat from ★ across, dc in
last dc: 17 dc and 14 7-tr groups.

Repeat Rows 3 and 4 for pattern, until Afghan Body
measures approximately 43" from beginning ch, ending
by working Row 3.

Last Row: Ch 3, turn; dc in closing ch of next Popcorn
and in next tr, ★ hdc in next tr, sc in next 3 tr, hdc in next
tr, dc in next tr, dc in closing ch of next Popcorn and in
next st; repeat from ★ across; do **not** finish off: 115 sts.

EDGING
Rnd 1: Ch 1, turn; 2 sc in first dc, sc in next dc and in
each st across to last dc, 3 sc in last dc; work 161 sc
evenly spaced across end of rows; working in sps and in
free loops of beginning ch *(Fig. 3, page 1)*, 3 sc in first
ch, sc in next ch, (3 sc in next sp, sc in next ch) across to
marked ch, 3 sc in marked ch; work 161 sc evenly
spaced across end of rows; sc in same st as first sc; join
with slip st to first sc: 560 sc.

Rnd 2 (Eyelet rnd)**:** Ch 6 **(counts as first dc plus
ch 3)**, do **not** turn; dc in same st, ch 1, ★ skip next sc,
(dc in next sc, ch 1, skip next sc) across to center sc of
next corner 3-sc group, (dc, ch 3, dc) in center sc, ch 1;
repeat from ★ 2 times **more**, skip next sc, (dc in next sc,
ch 1, skip next sc) across; join with slip st to first dc:
284 dc and 284 sps.

Rnd 3: Slip st in first corner ch-3 sp, ch 4, 8 tr in same
sp, ★ † skip next dc, work Popcorn in next dc, skip next
dc, (7 tr in next dc, skip next dc, work Popcorn in next
dc, skip next dc) across to next corner ch-3 sp †, 9 tr in
corner ch-3 sp; repeat from ★ 2 times **more**, then repeat
from † to † once; join with slip st to top of beginning
ch-4, finish off.

Design by Sarah Anne Phillips.

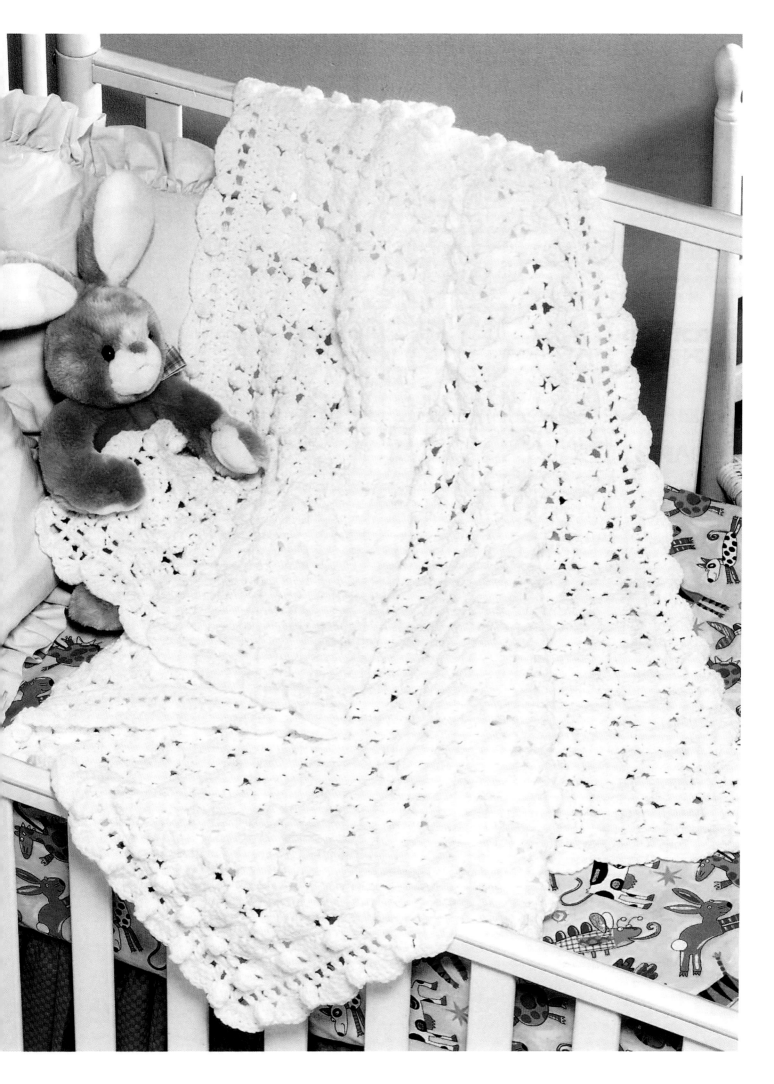

ANGEL WINGS

Finished Size: 36" x 44½"

MATERIALS

Sport Weight Yarn:
   23 ounces, (650 grams, 2,300 yards)
Crochet hook, size G (4.00 mm) **or** size needed
   for gauge
Yarn needle

GAUGE: Each Square = 8¾"

Gauge Swatch: 2½" square
Work same as Square through Rnd 2.

STITCH GUIDE

> **POPCORN**
> 4 Dc in st or sp indicated, drop loop from hook,
> insert hook in first dc of 4-dc group, hook dropped
> loop and draw through, ch 1 to close.

SQUARE (Make 20)

Ch 5; join with slip st to form a ring.

Rnd 1 (Right side)**:** Ch 3 **(counts as first dc, now and throughout)**, 2 dc in ring, (ch 3, 3 dc in ring) 3 times, ch 1, hdc in first dc to form last ch-3 sp: 12 dc and 4 ch-3 sps.

Note: Loop a short piece of yarn around any stitch to mark Rnd 1 as **right** side.

Rnd 2: Ch 3, 2 dc in last ch-3 sp made, ch 1, ★ (3 dc, ch 3, 3 dc) in next ch-3 sp, ch 1; repeat from ★ 2 times **more**, 3 dc in same sp as first dc, ch 1, hdc in first dc to form last ch-3 sp: 24 dc and 8 sps.

Rnd 3: Ch 3, 2 dc in last ch-3 sp made, (dc, work Popcorn, dc) in next ch-1 sp, ★ (3 dc, ch 3, 3 dc) in next corner ch-3 sp, (dc, work Popcorn, dc) in next ch-1 sp; repeat from ★ 2 times **more**, 3 dc in same sp as first dc, ch 1, hdc in first dc to form last ch-3 sp: 32 dc and 4 Popcorns.

Rnd 4: Ch 3, dc in last ch-3 sp made, ★ † dc in next 3 dc, work Popcorn in next dc, dc in closing ch of next Popcorn, work Popcorn in next dc, dc in next 3 dc †, (2 dc, ch 3, 2 dc) in next corner ch-3 sp; repeat from ★ 2 times **more**, then repeat from † to † once, 2 dc in same sp as first dc, ch 1, hdc in first dc to form last ch-3 sp: 44 dc and 8 Popcorns.

Rnd 5: Ch 3, dc in last ch-3 sp made, ★ † dc in next 4 dc, work Popcorn in next dc, (dc in closing ch of next Popcorn, work Popcorn in next dc) twice, dc in next 4 dc †, (2 dc, ch 3, 2 dc) in next corner ch-3 sp; repeat from ★ 2 times **more**, then repeat from † to † once, 2 dc in same sp as first dc, ch 1, hdc in first dc to form last ch-3 sp: 56 dc and 12 Popcorns.

Rnd 6: Ch 3, dc in last ch-3 sp made, ★ † dc in next 6 dc and in closing ch of next Popcorn, (work Popcorn in next dc, dc in closing ch of next Popcorn) twice, dc in next 6 dc †, (2 dc, ch 3, 2 dc) in next corner ch-3 sp; repeat from ★ 2 times **more**, then repeat from † to † once, 2 dc in same sp as first dc, ch 1, hdc in first dc to form last ch-3 sp: 76 dc and 8 Popcorns.

Rnd 7: Ch 3, dc in last ch-3 sp made, ★ † dc in next 9 dc and in closing ch of next Popcorn, work Popcorn in next dc, dc in closing ch of next Popcorn and in next 9 dc †, (2 dc, ch 3, 2 dc) in next corner ch-3 sp; repeat from ★ 2 times **more**, then repeat from † to † once, 2 dc in same sp as first dc, ch 1, hdc in first dc to form last ch-3 sp: 96 dc and 4 Popcorns.

Rnd 8: Ch 3, dc in last ch-3 sp made, ★ † dc in next dc, (skip next 2 dc, 3 dc in next dc) 3 times, skip next 2 dc, 3 dc in closing ch of next Popcorn, (skip next 2 dc, 3 dc in next dc) 3 times, skip next 2 dc, dc in next dc †, (2 dc, ch 3, 2 dc) in next corner ch-3 sp; repeat from ★ 2 times **more**, then repeat from † to † once, 2 dc in same sp as first dc, ch 1, hdc in first dc to form last ch-3 sp: 108 dc and 4 ch-3 sps.

Rnd 9: Ch 1, 3 sc in last ch-3 sp made, (sc in each dc across to next corner ch-3 sp, 5 sc in corner ch-3 sp) 3 times, sc in each dc across, 2 sc in same sp as first sc; join with slip st to first sc, finish off: 128 sc.

ASSEMBLY

Working through **both** loops, whipstitch Squares together forming 4 vertical strips of 5 Squares each *(Fig. 5a, page 2)*, beginning in center sc of first corner 5-sc group and ending in center sc of next corner 5-sc group; whipstitch strips together in same manner.

EDGING

With **right** side facing, join yarn with sc in center sc of any corner 5-sc group *(see Joining With Sc, page 1)*; ch 3, 2 dc in same st, [skip next 2 sc, (sc, ch 3, 2 dc) in next sc] 10 times, ★ † (sc, ch 3, 2 dc) in same st as joining on next Square, [skip next 2 sc, (sc, ch 3, 2 dc) in next sc] 10 times †; repeat from † to † across to within one sc of center sc of next corner 5-sc group, skip next sc, (sc, ch 3, 2 dc) in center sc, [skip next 2 sc, (sc, ch 3, 2 dc) in next sc] 10 times; repeat from ★ 2 times **more**, then repeat from † to † across to last sc, skip last sc; join with slip st to first sc, finish off.

Design by Geneva Warren.

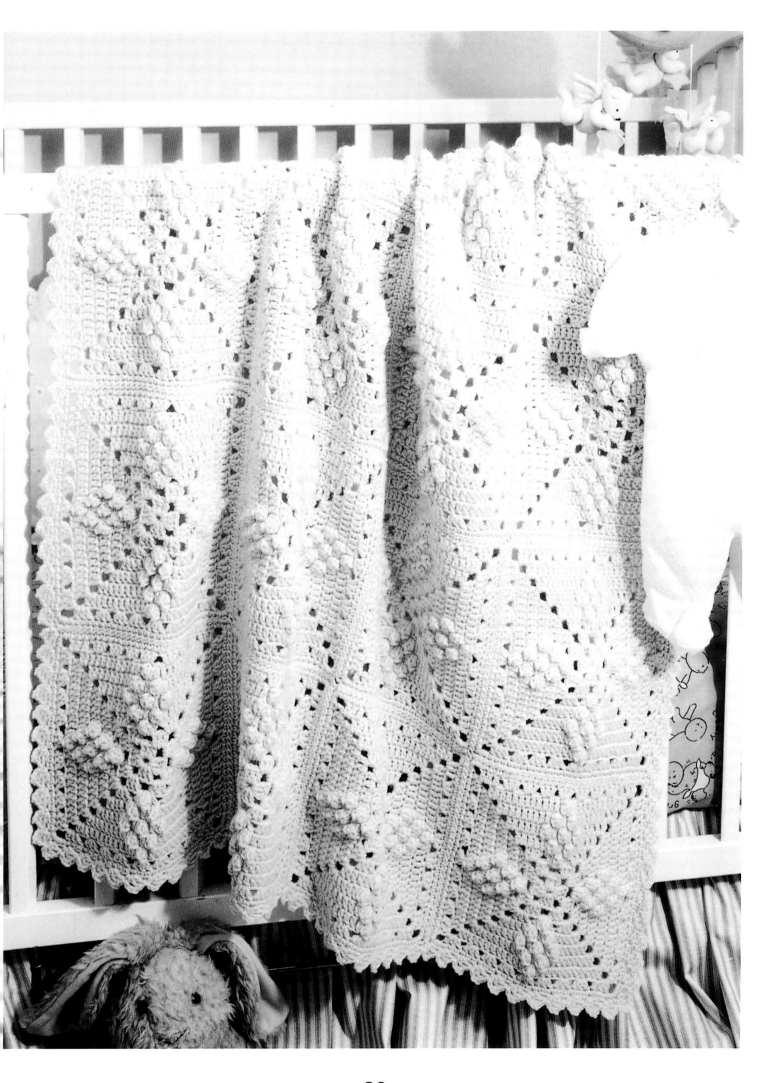

LOTS OF HUGS

Finished Size: 38½" x 50½"

MATERIALS

Sport Weight Yarn:
   White - 21½ ounces, (610 grams, 1,720 yards)
   Green - 11 ounces, (310 grams, 880 yards)
Crochet hook, size E (3.50 mm) **or** size needed
   for gauge

GAUGE: In pattern, 21 dc = 4"; Rows 2-19 = 7¼"

Gauge Swatch: 4¾"w x 4"h
With Green, ch 27 **loosely**.
Work same as Afghan Body for 10 rows.
Finish off.

Each row is worked across length of Afghan.

STITCH GUIDE

TREBLE CROCHET (abbreviated tr)
YO twice, insert hook in st indicated, YO and pull up
a loop (4 loops on hook), (YO and draw through
2 loops on hook) 3 times.

SPLIT TREBLE CROCHET
   (abbreviated Split tr)
First Leg: YO twice, insert hook in same st as last
sc made, YO and pull up a loop (4 loops on hook),
(YO and draw through 2 loops on hook) twice
(2 loops remaining on hook).

Second Leg: YO twice, insert hook in st indicated,
YO and pull up a loop, (YO and draw through
2 loops on hook) twice, YO and draw through all
3 loops on hook.

AFGHAN BODY

With Green, ch 267 **loosely**.

Row 1 (Right side)**:** Dc in back ridge of fourth ch from
hook *(Fig. 1, page 1)* and each ch across **(3 skipped
chs count as first dc)**: 265 dc.

Note: Loop a short piece of yarn around any stitch to
mark Row 1 as **right** side.

Row 2: Ch 1, turn; sc in first dc, ★ ch 3, work First Leg
of Split tr, skip next 5 dc, (work Second Leg of Split tr,
ch 3, sc) in next dc; repeat from ★ across: 44 Split tr and
45 sc.

Row 3: Ch 4, turn; (tr, ch 3, sc) in next Split tr, ch 3,
work First Leg of Split tr, ★ (work Second Leg of Split tr,
ch 3, sc) in next Split tr, ch 3, work First Leg of Split tr;
repeat from ★ across to last sc, work Second Leg of
Split tr in last sc: 44 Split tr and one tr.

Row 4: Ch 1, turn; sc in first Split tr, ch 5, (sc in next
Split tr, ch 5) across to last tr, sc in last tr: 45 sc and
44 ch-5 sps.

Row 5: Ch 3 **(counts as first dc, now and
throughout)**, turn; (5 dc in next ch-5 sp, dc in next sc)
across: 265 dc.

Finish off.

Row 6: With **right** side facing, join White with dc in first
dc *(see Joining With Dc, page 1)*; dc in next dc and in
each dc across.

Rows 7-18: Repeat Rows 2-5, 3 times.

Finish off.

Row 19: With **right** side facing, join Green with dc in
first dc; dc in next dc and in each dc across.

Rows 20-95: Repeat Rows 2-19, 4 times; then repeat
Rows 2-5 once **more**.

Finish off.

FRINGE

Cut a piece of cardboard 5" x 8". Wind the yarn **loosely**
and **evenly** around the cardboard lengthwise until the
card is filled, then cut across one end; repeat as needed.
Hold together 6 strands of corresponding color yarn; fold
in half.
With **wrong** side facing and using a crochet hook, draw
the folded end up through a row and pull the loose ends
through the folded end *(Fig. 10a)*; draw the knot up
tightly *(Fig. 10b)*. Repeat, spacing as desired or using
photo as a guide.
Lay flat on a hard surface and trim the ends.

Fig. 10a

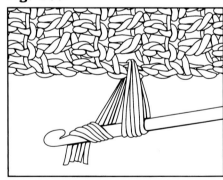

Fig. 10b

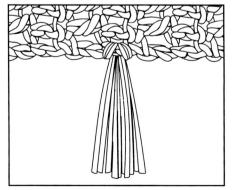

Design by Pat Gibbons.

HEIRLOOM TREASURE

Finished Size: 40" square

MATERIALS
Baby Fingering Weight Yarn:
20 ounces, (570 grams, 3,085 yards)
Crochet hook, size C (2.75 mm) **or** size needed
for gauge
1/4"w Ribbon - 8 yards
Sewing needle and thread

GAUGE: 24 dc = 4"

Gauge Swatch: 3 1/2" square
Work same as Afghan Body through Rnd 5.

AFGHAN BODY
Ch 4; join with slip st to form a ring.

Rnd 1 (Right side)**:** Ch 3 **(counts as first dc, now and throughout)**, 2 dc in ring, (ch 4, 3 dc in ring) 3 times, ch 2, hdc in first dc to form last ch-4 sp: 12 dc and 4 ch-4 sps.

Note: Loop a short piece of yarn around any stitch to mark Rnd 1 as **right** side.

Rnds 2-8: Ch 3, dc in last ch-4 sp made and in each dc across to next corner ch-4 sp, ★ (2 dc, ch 4, 2 dc) in corner ch-4 sp, dc in each dc across to next corner ch-4 sp; repeat from ★ 2 times **more**, 2 dc in same sp as first dc, ch 2, hdc in first dc to form last ch-4 sp: 124 dc and 4 ch-4 sps.

Rnd 9 (Eyelet rnd)**:** Ch 4 **(counts as first dc plus ch 1)**, dc in last ch-4 sp made, ch 1, skip next dc, (dc in next dc, ch 1, skip next dc) across to next corner ch-4 sp, ★ (dc, ch 1, dc, ch 4, dc, ch 1, dc) in corner ch-4 sp, ch 1, skip next dc, (dc in next dc, ch 1, skip next dc) across to next corner ch-4 sp; repeat from ★ 2 times **more**, (dc, ch 1, dc) in same sp as first dc, ch 2, hdc in first dc to form last ch-4 sp: 76 dc and 76 sps.

Rnd 10: Ch 3, dc in last ch-4 sp made and in each dc and each ch-1 sp across to next corner ch-4 sp, ★ (2 dc, ch 4, 2 dc) in corner ch-4 sp, dc in each dc and in each ch-1 sp across to next corner ch-4 sp; repeat from ★ 2 times **more**, 2 dc in same sp as first dc, ch 2, hdc in first dc to form last ch-4 sp: 164 dc and 4 ch-4 sps.

Rnds 11-25: Ch 3, dc in last ch-4 sp made and in each dc across to next corner ch-4 sp, ★ (2 dc, ch 4, 2 dc) in corner ch-4 sp, dc in each dc across to next corner ch-4 sp; repeat from ★ 2 times **more**, 2 dc in same sp as first dc, ch 2, hdc in first dc to form last ch-4 sp: 404 dc and 4 ch-4 sps.

Rnd 26 (Eyelet rnd)**:** Repeat Rnd 9: 216 dc and 216 sps.

Rnd 27: Repeat Rnd 10: 444 dc and 4 ch-4 sps.

Rnds 28-43: Ch 3, dc in last ch-4 sp made and in each dc across to next corner ch-4 sp, ★ (2 dc, ch 4, 2 dc) in corner ch-4 sp, dc in each dc across to next corner ch-4 sp; repeat from ★ 2 times **more**, 2 dc in same sp as first dc, ch 2, hdc in first dc to form last ch-4 sp: 700 dc and 4 ch-4 sps.

Rnd 44 (Eyelet rnd)**:** Repeat Rnd 9; do **not** finish off: 364 dc and 364 sps.

RUFFLE
Rnd 1: Ch 1, sc in last ch-4 sp made and in next dc, ★ † sc in next ch-1 sp, ch 5, sc in next dc, ch 5, sc in next ch-1 sp, ch 5, sc in next dc, sc in next ch-1 sp and in next dc, ch 5, sc in next ch-1 sp, ch 5, sc in next dc, ch 5, sc in next ch-1 sp and in next dc †; repeat from † to † across to next corner ch-4 sp, sc in corner ch-4 sp, (ch 5, sc in same sp) 3 times, sc in next dc; repeat from ★ 2 times **more**, then repeat from † to † across, (sc, ch 5) 3 times in same sp as first sc; join with slip st to first sc: 444 ch-5 sps.

Rnd 2: Slip st in next sc, ch 3, 2 dc in same st, ch 3, sc in next ch-5 sp, 9 dc in next ch-5 sp, sc in next ch-5 sp, ch 3, skip next sc, ★ 3 dc in next sc, ch 3, sc in next ch-5 sp, 9 dc in next ch-5 sp, sc in next ch-5 sp, ch 3, skip next sc; repeat from ★ around; join with slip st to first dc: 148 9-dc groups.

Rnd 3: Ch 1, sc in same st and in next 2 dc, ch 1, skip next sc, (dc in next dc, ch 1) 9 times, skip next sc, ★ sc in next 3 dc, ch 1, skip next sc, (dc in next dc, ch 1) 9 times, skip next sc; repeat from ★ around; join with slip st to first sc.

Rnd 4: Slip st in next sc, ch 1, sc in same st, skip next sc, (dc in next dc, ch 1) 4 times, (dc, ch 1, dc) in next dc, (ch 1, dc in next dc) 4 times, skip next sc, ★ sc in next sc, skip next sc, (dc in next dc, ch 1) 4 times, (dc, ch 1, dc) in next dc, (ch 1, dc in next dc) 4 times, skip next sc; repeat from ★ around; join with slip st to first sc.

Rnd 5: Ch 6 **(counts as first dc plus ch 3)**, skip next 2 dc, sc in next dc, ch 5, (skip next ch-1 sp, sc in next ch-1 sp, ch 5) twice, skip next dc, sc in next dc, ch 3, skip next 2 dc, ★ dc in next sc, ch 3, skip next 2 dc, sc in next dc, ch 5, (skip next ch-1 sp, sc in next ch-1 sp, ch 5) twice, skip next dc, sc in next dc, ch 3, skip next 2 dc; repeat from ★ around; join with slip st to first dc.

Rnd 6: Ch 3, 2 dc in same st, ch 3, skip next ch-3 sp, sc in next ch-5 sp, 9 dc in next ch-5 sp, sc in next ch-5 sp, ch 3, skip next sc, ★ 3 dc in next dc, ch 3, skip next ch-3 sp, sc in next ch-5 sp, 9 dc in next ch-5 sp, sc in next ch-5 sp, ch 3, skip next sc; repeat from ★ around; join with slip st to first dc: 148 9-dc groups.

Rnds 7-16: Repeat Rnds 3-6 twice, then repeat Rnds 3 and 4 once **more**; at end of Rnd 16, do **not** finish off.

Continued on page 25.

24

Rnd 17: Ch 1, sc in same st and in next ch-1 sp, (ch 3, sc in next ch-1 sp) 8 times, skip next dc, ★ sc in next sc and in next ch-1 sp, (ch 3, sc in next ch-1 sp) 8 times, skip next dc; repeat from ★ around; join with slip st to first sc, finish off.

Using photo as a guide, weave ribbon through corner ch-4 sps diagonally across Afghan Body, leaving a short length at each end; tack in place at corners. Weave a ribbon through Eyelets across each side on Rnd 44 of Afghan Body, and tie in a bow at each corner.

Design by Joan E. Reeves.

BABY LOVE

Finished Size: 39½" x 44½"

MATERIALS
Sport Weight Yarn:
  White - 15 ounces, (430 grams, 1,200 yards)
  Blue - 3½ ounces, (100 grams, 280 yards)
  Pink - 2½ ounces, (70 grams, 200 yards)
Crochet hook, size F (3.75 mm) **or** size needed
  for gauge

GAUGE SWATCH: 1¾" diameter
Work same as First Motif.

FIRST MOTIF
Rnd 1 (Right side): With White, ch 5, hdc in fifth ch from hook, ch 2, (hdc in same ch, ch 2) 6 times; join with slip st to third ch of beginning ch-5: 8 sts and 8 ch-2 sps.

Note: Loop a short piece of yarn around any stitch to mark Rnd 1 as **right** side.

Rnd 2: Ch 1, sc in same st, ch 3, (sc in next hdc, ch 3) around; join with slip st to first sc, finish off: 8 sc and 8 ch-3 sps.

ADDITIONAL MOTIFS
Note: The method used to connect the Motifs is a no-sew joining also known as "join-as-you-go". After the first Motif is made, each remaining Motif is worked through Rnd 1, then crocheted together as Rnd 2 is worked *(Fig. 6, page 2)*.

Following Placement Diagram, make Motifs using color indicated.

Rnd 1: Work same as First Motif: 8 sts and 8 ch-2 sps.

Note: Mark Rnd 1 as **right** side.

Rnd 2 (Joining rnd): Work One or Two Side Joining as needed.

ONE SIDE JOINING
Rnd 2 (Joining rnd): Ch 1, sc in same st, (ch 3, sc in next hdc) 6 times, ch 1, holding Motifs with **wrong** sides together, slip st in center ch of corresponding ch-3 on **adjacent Motif**, ch 1, sc in next hdc on **new Motif**, ch 1, slip st in center ch of next ch-3 on **adjacent Motif**, ch 1; join with slip st to first sc on **new Motif**, finish off.

TWO SIDE JOINING
Rnd 2 (Joining rnd): Ch 1, sc in same st, (ch 3, sc in next hdc) 4 times, ch 1, holding Motifs with **wrong** sides together, (slip st in center ch of corresponding ch-3 on **adjacent Motif**, ch 1, sc in next hdc on **new Motif**, ch 1) twice, slip st in center ch of next unworked ch-3 on **adjacent Motif**, ch 1, sc in next hdc on **new Motif**, ch 1, slip st in center ch of next ch-3 on **adjacent Motif**, ch 1; join with slip st to first sc on **new Motif**, finish off.

PLACEMENT DIAGRAM

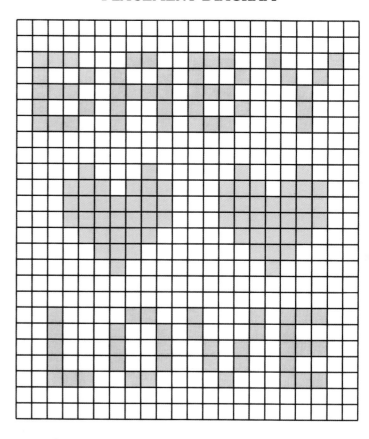

EDGING
With **right** side facing and working in unworked ch-3 sps, join Blue with sc in any ch-3 sp *(see Joining With Sc, page 1)*; ch 3, dc in third ch from hook, ★ sc in next ch-3 sp, ch 3, dc in third ch from hook; repeat from ★ around; join with slip st to first sc, finish off.

Design by Carole G. Wilder.

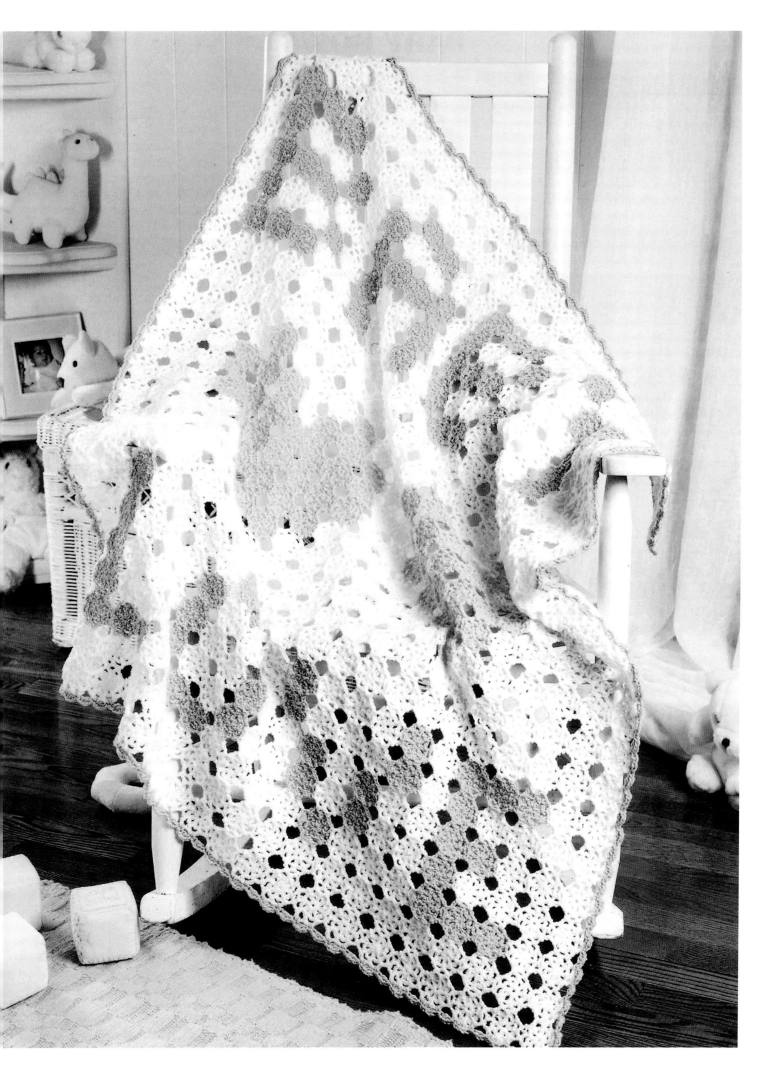

BABY BOWS

Finished Size: 37" x 52½"

MATERIALS

Sport Weight Yarn:
    White - 19 ounces, (540 grams, 1,520 yards)
    Green - 19 ounces, (540 grams, 1,520 yards)
Crochet hook, size E (3.50 mm) **or** size needed
    for gauge
¼"w Ribbon - 5 yards
Sewing needle and thread

It is strongly recommended that you complete the Gauge Swatch to practice the pattern and the Bows instructions before you begin the Afghan.

GAUGE: 18 sc and 19 rows = 4"

Gauge Swatch: 6½"w x 2"h
With White, ch 31 **loosely**.
Work same as Afghan Body for 9 rows.
Finish off.

CHANGING COLORS

Insert hook in next sc, YO and pull up a loop, drop yarn to **right** side, with new color, YO and draw through both loops on hook *(Fig. 4, page 2)*. Do **not** cut yarn unless otherwise instructed.

Note: Pick up new color, holding yarn **loosely** across **right** side of work. Be careful **not** to work over carried yarn.

AFGHAN BODY

With White, ch 151 **loosely**.

Row 1 (Right side)**:** Sc in second ch from hook and in each ch across changing to Green in last sc: 150 sc.

Note: Loop a short piece of yarn around any stitch to mark Row 1 as **right** side.

Rows 2-9: With Green, ch 1, turn; sc in first 9 sc, sc in next sc changing to White, ★ sc in next 9 sc, sc in next sc changing colors; repeat from ★ across.

Rows 10-17: With White, ch 1, turn; sc in first 9 sc, sc in next sc changing to Green, ★ sc in next 9 sc, sc in next sc changing colors; repeat from ★ across.

Rows 18-233: Repeat Rows 2-17, 13 times; then repeat Rows 2-9 once **more**; at end of Row 233, finish off both colors.

EDGING

Foundation: With **right** side facing and working in end of rows, join White with sc in Row 1 *(see Joining With Sc, page 1)*; sc in next row and in each row across to last row, skip last row; working in sts across Row 233, 3 sc in first sc, skip next sc, sc in next sc and in each sc across to last sc, 3 sc in last sc; working in end of rows, skip first row, sc in next row and in each row across, leave remaining sts unworked: 617 sc.

Rnd 1: Ch 1, turn; (sc in each sc across to center sc of next corner 3-sc group, 3 sc in center sc) twice, sc in next sc and in each sc across; working in free loops of beginning ch *(Fig. 3, page 1)*, 3 sc in ch at base of first sc, sc in next ch and in each ch across to last 2 chs, 2 sc in next ch, 3 sc in last ch; join with slip st to first sc, finish off: 776 sc.

Rnd 2: With **right** side facing, join Green with sc in center sc of any corner 3-sc group; sc in same st and in each sc around working 3 sc in center sc of each corner 3-sc group, sc in same st as first sc; join with slip st to first sc: 784 sc.

Rnd 3 (Eyelet rnd)**:** Ch 4 **(counts as first dc plus ch 1)**, do **not** turn; dc in same st, ch 1, ★ skip next sc, (dc in next sc, ch 1, skip next sc) across to center sc of next corner 3-sc group, (dc, ch 1) 3 times in center sc; repeat from ★ 2 times **more**, skip next sc, (dc in next sc, ch 1, skip next sc) across, dc in same st as first dc, ch 1; join with slip st to first dc: 400 dc and 400 ch-1 sps.

Rnd 4: Ch 1, 3 sc in same st, sc in each ch-1 sp and in each dc around working 3 sc in center dc of each corner 3-dc group; join with slip st to first sc, finish off: 808 sc.

Rnd 5: With **right** side facing, join White with sc in center sc of any corner 3-sc group; sc in same st and in each sc around working 3 sc in center sc of each corner 3-sc group, sc in same st as first sc; join with slip st to first sc: 816 sc.

Rnd 6: Ch 1, sc in same st, ch 5, slip st in third ch from hook, ch 2, skip next 2 sc, ★ sc in next sc, ch 5, slip st in third ch from hook, ch 2, skip next 2 sc; repeat from ★ around; join with slip st to first sc, finish off.

BOWS

Cut 8" lengths of each color yarn. With **right** side facing and using photo as a guide for placement, tie a bow with a strand of matching color yarn around group of strands in front of each block. Trim bow as desired.

Using photo as a guide, weave ribbon through Eyelet rnd and tack ends to wrong side.

Design by Elsie Bugosh.

BRIGHT EYES

Finished Size: 33¹/₂" x 46"

MATERIALS
Worsted Weight Yarn:
    19 ounces, (540 grams, 1,245 yards)
Crochet hook, size H (5.00 mm) **or** size needed
    for gauge

GAUGE: In pattern, one repeat = 3"; 6 rows = 4"

Gauge Swatch: 5¹/₂"w x 4³/₄"h
Ch 23.
Work same as Afghan Body for 7 rows.
Finish off.

AFGHAN BODY
Ch 131, place marker in sixth ch from hook for
st placement.

Row 1 (Right side)**:** Dc in fourth ch from hook
(3 skipped chs count as first dc), skip next 2 chs,
(3 dc, ch 2, 3 dc) in next ch, ★ skip next 2 chs, dc in next
ch, ch 5, skip next 5 chs, dc in next ch, skip next 2 chs,
(3 dc, ch 2, 3 dc) in next ch; repeat from ★ across to last
4 chs, skip next 2 chs, dc in last 2 chs: 90 dc and 21 sps.

Note: Loop a short piece of yarn around any stitch to
mark Row 1 as **right** side.

Row 2: Ch 3 **(counts as first dc, now and
throughout)**, turn; dc in next dc, (3 dc, ch 2, 3 dc) in
next ch-2 sp, ★ skip next 3 dc, dc in next dc, dc in next
5 chs and in next dc, (3 dc, ch 2, 3 dc) in next ch-2 sp;
repeat from ★ across to last 5 dc, skip next 3 dc, dc in
last 2 dc: 140 dc and 11 ch-2 sps.

Row 3: Ch 3, turn; dc in next dc, (3 dc, ch 2, 3 dc) in
next ch-2 sp, ★ ch 2, skip next 5 dc, dc in next 3 dc,
(ch 2, 3 dc) twice in next ch-2 sp; repeat from ★ across to
last 5 dc, skip next 3 dc, dc in last 2 dc: 100 dc and
31 ch-2 sps.

Row 4: Ch 3, turn; dc in next dc, (3 dc, ch 2, 3 dc) in
next ch-2 sp, ★ skip next 3 dc, dc in next ch, ch 5, skip
next 3 dc and next ch, dc in next ch, (3 dc, ch 2, 3 dc) in
next ch-2 sp; repeat from ★ across to last 5 dc, skip next
3 dc, dc in last 2 dc: 90 dc and 21 sps.

Row 5: Ch 3, turn; dc in next dc, (3 dc, ch 2, 3 dc) in
next ch-2 sp, ★ skip next 3 dc, dc in next dc, dc in next
5 chs and in next dc, (3 dc, ch 2, 3 dc) in next ch-2 sp;
repeat from ★ across to last 5 dc, skip next 3 dc, dc in
last 2 dc: 140 dc and 11 ch-2 sps.

Rows 6-67: Repeat Rows 3-5, 20 times; then repeat
Rows 3 and 4 once **more**; at end of Row 67, do **not**
finish off.

EDGING
Ch 3, do **not** turn; working in end of rows, (dc, ch 2,
3 dc) in end of Row 67, [skip next 2 rows, (3 dc, ch 2,
3 dc) in next row] across to last 3 rows, skip next 2 rows,
(3 dc, ch 2, dc) in last row; working in free loops of
beginning ch *(Fig. 3, page 1)*, dc in first 2 chs, skip next
2 chs, (3 dc, ch 2, 3 dc) in next ch, ★ skip next 2 chs, dc
in next ch, skip next 2 chs, 3 dc in next ch, skip next
2 chs, dc in next ch, skip next 2 chs, (3 dc, ch 2, 3 dc) in
next ch; repeat from ★ across to marked ch, skip marked
ch and next ch, dc in next 2 chs; working in end of rows,
(dc, ch 2, 3 dc) in first row, [skip next 2 rows, (3 dc, ch 2,
3 dc) in next row] across to last 3 rows, skip next 2 rows,
(3 dc, ch 2, dc) in last row; working across Row 67, dc in
first 2 dc, (3 dc, ch 2, 3 dc) in next ch-2 sp, skip next
3 dc, dc in next dc, † skip next 2 chs, 3 dc in next ch, dc
in next dc, (3 dc, ch 2, 3 dc) in next ch-2 sp, skip next
3 dc, dc in next dc †; repeat from † to † across; join with
slip st to first dc, finish off.

Design by Kathy Missett.

BABY BLOCKS

Finished Size: 35" x 46"

MATERIALS
Worsted Weight Yarn:
- White - 7 ounces, (200 grams, 395 yards)
- Yellow - 4½ ounces, (130 grams, 255 yards)
- Green - 4½ ounces, (130 grams, 255 yards)
- Blue - 4½ ounces, (130 grams, 255 yards)
- Purple - 4½ ounces, (130 grams, 255 yards)
- Pink - 4½ ounces, (130 grams, 255 yards)
- Orange - 4½ ounces, (130 grams, 255 yards)

Crochet hook, size H (5.00 mm) **or** size needed for gauge

GAUGE: 11 dc and 6 rows = 3"

Gauge Swatch: 3" square
Work same as Strip A through Row 6.

COLOR SEQUENCES
STRIP A (Make 2)
6 Rows **each** color: Pink, Purple, Blue, Green, Yellow, Orange, Pink, Purple, Pink, Orange, Yellow, Green, Blue, Purple, Pink.

STRIP B (Make 2)
6 Rows **each** color: Purple, Blue, Green, Yellow, Orange, Pink, Purple, Blue, Purple, Pink, Orange, Yellow, Green, Blue, Purple.

STRIP C (Make 2)
6 Rows **each** color: Blue, Green, Yellow, Orange, Pink, Purple, Blue, Green, Blue, Purple, Pink, Orange, Yellow, Green, Blue.

STRIP D (Make 2)
6 Rows **each** color: Green, Yellow, Orange, Pink, Purple, Blue, Green, Yellow, Green, Blue, Purple, Pink, Orange, Yellow, Green.

STRIP E (Make 2)
6 Rows **each** color: Yellow, Orange, Pink, Purple, Blue, Green, Yellow, Orange, Yellow, Green, Blue, Purple, Pink, Orange, Yellow.

STRIP F (Make 1)
6 Rows **each** color: Orange, Pink, Purple, Blue, Green, Yellow, Orange, Pink, Orange, Yellow, Green, Blue, Purple, Pink, Orange.

STRIP (Make 11)
With color indicated, ch 13 **loosely**.

Row 1 (Right side)**:** Dc in fourth ch from hook **(3 skipped chs count as first dc)** and in each ch across: 11 dc.

Note: Loop a short piece of yarn around any stitch to mark Row 1 as **right** side and bottom edge.

Row 2: Ch 3 **(counts as first dc, now and throughout)**, turn; dc in next dc and in each dc across.

Rows 3-5: Ch 3, turn; dc in next dc and in each dc across.

Row 6: Ch 3, turn; dc in next dc and in each dc across changing to next color in last dc *(Fig. 4, page 2)*; cut previous color.

Rows 7-11: Ch 3, turn; dc in next dc and in each dc across.

Row 12: Ch 3, turn; dc in next dc and in each dc across changing to next color in last dc; cut previous color.

Rows 13-90: Following Color Sequence, repeat Rows 7-12, 13 times; at the end of Row 90, do **not** change colors.

Finish off.

ASSEMBLY
Strip Sequence: Strip A, Strip B, Strip C, Strip D, Strip E, Strip F, Strip E, Strip D, Strip C, Strip B, Strip A.

Holding two Strips with **wrong** sides together, bottom edges at same end, and working in end of rows, join Strips together as follows:
Join White with slip st in Row 1 on front Strip; ch 1, slip st in first row on **next Strip**, ★ ch 1, slip st in next row on **next Strip**; repeat from ★ across; finish off.

Repeat for remaining Strips.

HORIZONTAL TRIM
With **right** side facing and working around posts of dc across **each** Strip, join White with slip st around first dc on Row 7; ch 1, skip first dc on Row 6, slip st around next dc, ch 1, skip next dc on Row 7, slip st around next dc, ★ ch 1, skip next dc on Row 6, slip st around next dc, ch 1, skip next dc on Row 7, slip st around next dc; repeat from ★ across.

Work remaining 13 Horizontal Trims in same manner across first row of next color blocks and last row of previous color blocks.

Continued on page 33

EDGING

Rnd 1: With **right** side facing and working across top edge, join White with sc in sp **after** first dc *(see Joining With Sc, page 1)*; ch 3, sc in same sp, † ch 1, (skip next 2 dc, sc in sp **before** next dc, ch 1) twice, skip next dc, dc in sp **before** next dc, ★ (ch 1, skip next 2 dc, sc in sp **before** next dc) twice, ch 2, skip next joining and next dc, sc in sp **before** next dc, ch 1, (skip next 2 dc, sc in sp **before** next dc, ch 1) twice, skip next dc, sc in sp **before** next dc; repeat from ★ 9 times **more**, ch 1, skip next 2 dc, sc in sp **before** next dc, ch 1, skip next 2 dc, (sc, ch 3, sc) in sp **before** last dc, ch 1 †; working in end of rows, (sc in next row, ch 1) across to last row, (sc, ch 3, sc) in last row; working around beginning ch and **between** dc on Row 1, repeat from † to † once; working in end of rows, (sc in next row, ch 1) across; join with slip st to first sc: 312 sc and 312 sps.

Rnd 2: Slip st in first corner ch-3 sp, ch 6, (dc, ch 3, dc in same sp, ★ skip next ch-1 sp, [(dc, ch 3, dc) in next sp, skip next ch-1 sp] across to next corner ch-3 sp, dc in corner ch-3 sp, (ch 3, dc in same sp) twice; repeat from ★ 2 times **more**, skip next ch-1 sp, [(dc, ch 3, dc) in next sp, skip next ch-1 sp] across; join with slip st to third ch of beginning ch-6, finish off.

Design by Susan Lowman.

JUST DUCKY

Finished Size: 31" x 45"

MATERIALS
Worsted Weight Yarn:
   17½ ounces, (500 grams, 1,150 yards)
Crochet hook, size K (6.50 mm) **or** size needed
   for gauge

GAUGE: In pattern, 3 repeats = 4¾"; 6 rows = 3½"

Gauge Swatch: 5" square
Ch 21.
Work same as Afghan Body for 8 rows.
Finish off.

AFGHAN BODY

Ch 111, place marker in third ch from hook for st placement.

Row 1 (Right side): (2 Dc, ch 1, 2 dc) in sixth ch from hook, skip next 2 chs, dc in next ch, ★ skip next 2 chs, (2 dc, ch 1, 2 dc) in next ch, skip next 2 chs, dc in next ch; repeat from ★ across: 90 dc and 18 ch-1 sps.

Note: Loop a short piece of yarn around any stitch to mark Row 1 as **right** side.

Row 2: Ch 3 **(counts as first dc, now and throughout)**, turn; (2 dc, ch 1, 2 dc) in next ch-1 sp, ★ skip next 2 dc, dc in next dc, (2 dc, ch 1, 2 dc) in next ch-1 sp; repeat from ★ across to last 2 dc, skip last 2 dc, dc in next ch: 91 dc and 18 ch-1 sps.

Row 3: Ch 3, turn; ★ (2 dc, ch 1, 2 dc) in next ch-1 sp, skip next 2 dc, dc in next dc; repeat from ★ across.

Repeat Row 3 until Afghan Body measures approximately 43" from beginning ch, ending by working a **right** side row.

Last Row: Ch 5, turn; sc in next ch-1 sp, ch 2, skip next 2 dc, dc in next dc, ★ ch 2, sc in next ch-1 sp, ch 2 skip next 2 dc, dc in next dc; repeat from ★ across; do **not** finish off: 37 sts and 36 sps.

EDGING

Rnd 1: Ch 8, turn; dc in first dc, ch 2, (skip next ch-2 sp, dc in next st, ch 2) across to last sp, skip next 2 chs, (dc, ch 5, dc) in next ch, ch 2; working across end of rows, (dc in top of next row, ch 2) across; working in free loops of beginning ch *(Fig. 3, page 1)*, (dc, ch 5, dc) in first ch, ch 2, skip next 2 chs, (dc in next ch, ch 2, skip next 2 chs) across to marked ch, (dc, ch 5, dc) in marked ch, ch 2; working across end of rows, dc in top of first row, ch 2, (dc in top of next row, ch 2) across; join with slip st to third ch of beginning ch-8.

Rnd 2: Slip st in first corner ch-5 sp, ch 4, dc in same sp, (ch 1, dc in same sp) 5 times, ★ † skip next dc, sc in next dc, [dc in next dc, (ch 1, dc in same st) 3 times, sc in next dc] across to within one dc of next corner ch-5 sp, skip next dc †, dc in corner ch-5 sp, (ch 1, dc in same sp) 6 times; repeat from ★ 2 times **more**, then repeat from † to † once; join with slip st to third ch of beginning ch-4, finish off.

Design by Marjorie Beach.

DAINTY FLOWERS

Finished Size: 37½" x 46"

MATERIALS

Worsted Weight Yarn:
- White - 16 ounces, (450 grams, 1,600 yards)
- Blue - 2 ounces, (60 grams, 200 yards)
- Pink - 2 ounces, (60 grams, 200 yards)
- Green - 2 ounces, (60 grams, 200 yards)
- Yellow - 2 ounces, (60 grams, 200 yards)

Crochet hook, size I (5.50 mm) **or** size needed for gauge

Yarn needle

GAUGE: Each Block = 8½"

Gauge Swatch: 3¼" square
Work same as Square A.

STITCH GUIDE

> **TREBLE CROCHET (abbreviated tr)**
> YO twice, insert hook in st or sp indicated, YO and pull up a loop (4 loops on hook), (YO and draw through 2 loops on hook) 3 times.
>
> **POPCORN**
> 3 Dc in sp indicated, drop loop from hook, insert hook in first dc of 3-dc group, hook dropped loop and draw through.

SQUARE (Make 80)

Referring to the table below, make 20 of **each** Square in the colors indicated.

	Square A	Square B	Square C	Square D
Rnd 1	Yellow	Green	Pink	Blue
Rnds 2 & 3	White	White	White	White

With color indicated, ch 4; join with slip st to form a ring.

Rnd 1 (Right side)**:** Ch 3 **(counts as first dc, now and throughout)**, 2 dc in ring, drop loop from hook, insert hook in first dc of 3-dc group, hook dropped loop and draw through **(beginning Popcorn made)**, ch 3, (work Popcorn in ring, ch 3) 3 times; join with slip st to top of Beginning Popcorn, finish off: 4 Popcorns and 4 ch-3 sps.

Note: Loop a short piece of yarn around any stitch to mark Rnd 1 as **right** side.

Rnd 2: With **right** side facing, join White with dc in any ch-3 sp *(see Joining With Dc, page 1)*; 2 dc in same sp, (3 dc, ch 2, 3 dc) in next 3 ch-3 sps, 3 dc in same sp as first dc, hdc in first dc to form last ch-2 sp: 24 dc and 4 ch-2 sps.

Rnd 3: Ch 3, (dc, ch 2, 2 dc) in last ch-2 sp made, (skip next dc, dc in sp **before** next dc) 5 times, ★ (2 dc, ch 2, 2 dc) in next corner ch-2 sp, (skip next dc, dc in sp **before** next dc) 5 times; repeat from ★ 2 times **more**; join with slip st to first dc, finish off: 36 dc and 4 ch-2 sps.

BLOCK (Make 20)

With White, using Block Diagram as a guide, and working through **inside** loops only, whipstitch 4 Squares together *(Fig. 5b, page 2)*, beginning in second ch of first corner ch-2 and ending in first ch of next corner ch-2.

BLOCK DIAGRAM

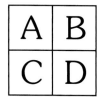

BORDER

Rnd 1: With **right** side facing, join White with dc in any corner ch-2 sp; dc in same sp, ★ † (skip next dc, dc in sp **before** next dc) 8 times, tr in corner sp on same Square, tr in next joining and in corner sp on next Square, (skip next dc, dc in sp **before** next dc) 8 times †, (2 dc, ch 1, 2 dc) in next corner ch-2 sp; repeat from ★ 2 times **more**, then repeat from † to † once, 2 dc in same sp as first dc, sc in first dc to form last ch-1 sp: 92 sts and 4 ch-1 sps.

Rnd 2: Ch 3, (dc, ch 1, 2 dc) in last ch-1 sp made, ★ (skip next st, dc in sp **before** next st) across to next corner ch-1 sp, (2 dc, ch 1, 2 dc) in corner ch-1 sp; repeat from ★ 2 times **more**, (skip next st, dc in sp **before** next st) across; join with slip st to first dc, finish off: 104 dc and 4 ch-1 sps.

Work Rnd 3, making 5 Blocks **each** in Pink, Blue, Green or Yellow.

Rnd 3: With **right** side facing, join color indicated with sc in any corner ch-1 sp *(see Joining With Sc, page 1)*; 2 sc in same sp, ★ (skip next dc, sc in sp **before** next dc) across to next corner ch-1 sp, 3 sc in corner ch-1 sp; repeat from ★ 2 times **more**, (skip next dc, sc in sp **before** next dc) across; join with slip st to first sc, finish off: 112 sc.

Continued on page 40

ANGEL SQUARES

Finished Size: 40" x 52½"

MATERIALS

Worsted Weight Yarn:
   White - 22½ ounces, (640 grams, 1,475 yards)
   Blue - 13 ounces, (370 grams, 850 yards)
Crochet hook, size G (4.00 mm) **or** size needed
   for gauge

GAUGE: Each Square = 12½"
            In pattern, 13 dc and 7 rows = 3"

Gauge Swatch: 3¼"w x 3½"h
Ch 16 **loosely**.
Row 1: Dc in fourth ch from hook **(3 skipped chs count as first dc)** and in each ch across: 14 dc.
Rows 2-8: Ch 3 **(counts as first dc)**, turn; dc in next dc and in each dc across.
Finish off.

SQUARE (Make 12)

With White, ch 45 **loosely**, place marker in third ch from hook for st placement.

Row 1 (Right side)**:** Dc in fourth ch from hook **(3 skipped chs count as first dc)** and in each ch across: 43 dc.

Note: Loop a short piece of yarn around any stitch to mark Row 1 as **right** side.

Row 2: Ch 3 **(counts as first dc, now and throughout)**, turn; dc in next 2 dc, ch 1, ★ skip next dc, dc in next dc, ch 1; repeat from ★ across to last 4 dc, skip next dc, dc in last 3 dc: 24 dc and 19 ch-1 sps.

Row 3: Ch 3, turn; dc in next 2 dc, ch 1, dc in next dc, (dc in next ch-1 sp and in next dc) across to last ch-1 sp, ch 1, skip last ch-1 sp, dc in last 3 dc: 41 dc and 2 ch-1 sps.

Angel is formed on Rows 4-21. Use color indicated, working over remaining color, carrying yarn with normal tension across top of previous row. Do **not** cut yarn until instructed.

Row 4: With White, ch 3, turn; working over Blue, dc in next 2 dc, ch 1, dc in next 17 dc changing to Blue in last dc made **(Fig. 4, page 2)**, dc in next 2 dc changing to White in last dc made, dc in next 16 dc, ch 1, dc in last 3 dc.

Continue to change color in same manner throughout.

Row 5: Ch 3, turn; dc in next 2 dc, ch 1, dc in next 7 dc, with Blue dc in next 20 dc, with White dc in next 8 dc, ch 1, dc in last 3 dc.

Row 6: Ch 3, turn; dc in next 2 dc, ch 1, dc in next 9 dc, with Blue dc in next 18 dc, with White dc in next 8 dc, ch 1, dc in last 3 dc.

Row 7: Ch 3, turn; dc in next 2 dc, ch 1, dc in next 9 dc, with Blue dc in next 16 dc, with White dc in next 10 dc, ch 1, dc in last 3 dc.

Row 8: Ch 3, turn; dc in next 2 dc, ch 1, dc in next 11 dc, with Blue dc in next 14 dc, with White dc in next 10 dc, ch 1, dc in last 3 dc.

Row 9: Ch 3, turn; dc in next 2 dc, ch 1, dc in next 11 dc, with Blue dc in next 12 dc, with White dc in next 12 dc, ch 1, dc in last 3 dc.

Row 10: Ch 3, turn; dc in next 2 dc, ch 1, dc in next 6 dc, with Blue dc in next 3 dc, with White dc in next 4 dc, with Blue dc in next 10 dc, with White dc in next 12 dc, ch 1, dc in last 3 dc.

Row 11: Ch 3, turn; dc in next 2 dc, ch 1, dc in next 13 dc, with Blue dc in next 8 dc, with White dc in next 3 dc, with Blue dc in next 4 dc, with White dc in next 7 dc, ch 1, dc in last 3 dc.

Row 12: Ch 3, turn; dc in next 2 dc, ch 1, dc in next 7 dc, with Blue dc in next 6 dc, with White dc in next 2 dc, with Blue dc in next 6 dc, with White dc in next 14 dc, ch 1, dc in last 3 dc.

Row 13: Ch 3, turn; dc in next 2 dc, ch 1, dc in next 14 dc, with Blue dc in next 13 dc, with White dc in next 8 dc, ch 1, dc in last 3 dc.

Row 14: Ch 3, turn; dc in next 2 dc, ch 1, dc in next 7 dc, with Blue dc in next 17 dc, with White dc in next 11 dc, ch 1, dc in last 3 dc.

Row 15: Ch 3, turn; dc in next 2 dc, ch 1, dc in next 11 dc, with Blue dc in next 2 dc, with White dc in next dc, with Blue dc in next 13 dc, with White dc in next 8 dc, ch 1, dc in last 3 dc.

Row 16: Ch 3, turn; dc in next 2 dc, ch 1, dc in next 8 dc, with Blue dc in next 7 dc, with White dc in next dc, with Blue dc in next 4 dc, with White dc in next 15 dc, ch 1, dc in last 3 dc.

Row 17: Ch 3, turn; dc in next 2 dc, ch 1, dc in next 14 dc, with Blue dc in next 6 dc, with White dc in next dc, with Blue dc in next 4 dc, with White dc in next 10 dc, ch 1, dc in last 3 dc.

Row 18: Ch 3, turn; dc in next 2 dc, ch 1, dc in next 15 dc, with Blue dc in next 6 dc, with White dc in next 14 dc, ch 1, dc in last 3 dc.

Row 19: Ch 3, turn; dc in next 2 dc, ch 1, dc in next 15 dc, with Blue dc in next 4 dc, with White dc in next 16 dc, ch 1, dc in last 3 dc.

Row 20: Ch 3, turn; dc in next 2 dc, ch 1, dc in each dc across to next ch-1 sp, ch 1, skip next ch-1 sp, dc in last 3 dc; do **not** finish off.

Continued on page 39

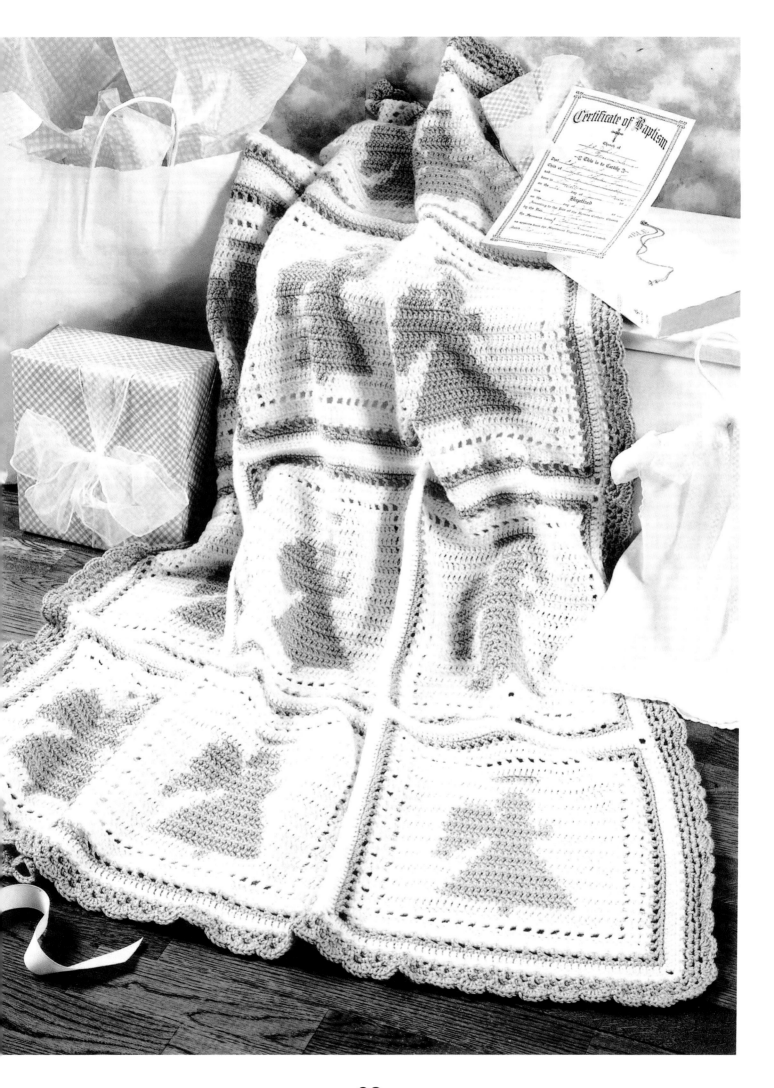

Row 21: Ch 3, turn; dc in next 2 dc, ch 1, dc in next 13 dc, with Blue dc in next 8 dc, with White dc in next 14 dc, ch 1, dc in last 3 dc; cut Blue.

Row 22: Ch 3, turn; dc in next 2 dc, ch 1, dc in each dc across to next ch-1 sp, ch 1, skip next ch-1 sp, dc in last 3 dc.

Row 23: Ch 3, turn; dc in next 2 dc, ch 1, dc in next dc, ch 1, ★ skip next dc, dc in next dc, ch 1; repeat from ★ across to next ch-1 sp, skip next ch-1 sp, dc in last 3 dc: 24 dc and 19 ch-1 sps.

Row 24: Ch 3, turn; dc in next dc and in each dc and each ch-1 sp across; do **not** finish off: 43 dc.

BORDER

Rnd 1: Ch 1, turn; 2 sc in first dc, sc in next dc and in each dc across to last dc, 3 sc in last dc; † working in end of rows, sc in first row, 2 sc in each of next 2 rows, sc in next row, (2 sc in each of next 3 rows, sc in next row) 5 times †; working in free loops of beginning ch *(Fig. 3, page 1)*, 3 sc in first ch, sc in next ch and in each ch across to marked ch, 3 sc in marked ch, repeat from † to † once, sc in same st as first sc; join with slip st to first sc, finish off: 176 sc.

Rnd 2: With **right** side facing, join Blue with dc in same st as joining *(see Joining With Dc, page 1)*; ch 3, dc in same st, ch 1, skip next sc, ★ (dc in next sc, ch 1, skip next sc) across to center sc of next corner 3-sc group, (dc, ch 3, dc) in center sc, ch 1, skip next sc; repeat from ★ 2 times **more**, (dc in next sc, ch 1, skip next sc) across; join with slip st to first dc: 92 dc and 92 sps.

Rnd 3: Ch 1, sc in same st, 3 sc in next corner ch-3 sp, ★ sc in each dc and in each ch-1 sp across to next corner ch-3 sp, 3 sc in corner ch-3 sp; repeat from ★ 2 times **more**, sc in each dc and in each ch-1 sp across; join with slip st to first sc, finish off: 192 sc.

Rnd 4: With **right** side facing, join White with dc in center sc of any corner 3-sc group; ch 3, dc in same st, ★ dc in next sc and in each sc across to center sc of next corner 3-sc group, (dc, ch 3, dc) in center sc; repeat from ★ 2 times **more**, dc in next sc and in each sc across; join with slip st to first dc, finish off: 196 dc and 4 ch-3 sps.

ASSEMBLY

Hold 2 Squares with **wrong** sides together and bottom edge of one Square to top edge of next Square. Working through **inside** loops on **both** pieces, join White with slip st in center ch of first corner ch-3; slip st in each st across ending in center ch of next corner ch-3; finish off.

Using Placement Diagram as a guide, join remaining Squares together in same manner forming 3 vertical strips of 4 Squares each; with bottom edge at same end, join strips together in same manner.

PLACEMENT DIAGRAM

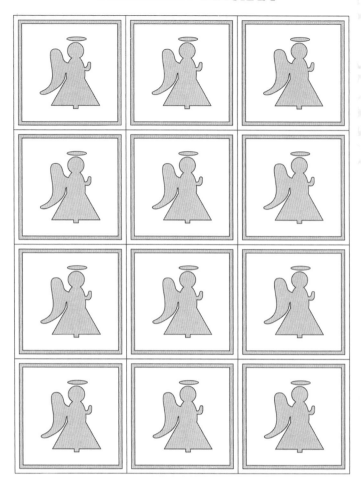

EDGING

Rnd 1: With **right** side facing, join White with sc in any corner ch-3 sp *(see Joining With Sc, page 1)*; 2 sc in same sp, sc in next 49 dc, ★ (2 sc in next sp, sc in next joining, 2 sc in next sp, sc in next 49 dc) across to next corner ch-3 sp, 3 sc in corner ch-3 sp, sc in next 49 dc; repeat from ★ 2 times **more**, (2 sc in next sp, sc in next joining, 2 sc in next sp, sc in next 49 dc) across; join with slip st to first sc, finish off: 748 sc.

Rnd 2: With **right** side facing, join Blue with sc in center sc of any corner 3-sc group; ch 3, skip next sc, ★ sc in next sc, ch 3, skip next sc; repeat from ★ around; join with slip st to first sc: 374 ch-3 sps.

Rnds 3 and 4: (Slip st, ch 1, sc) in first ch-3 sp, ch 3, (sc in next ch-3 sp, ch 3) around; join with slip st to first sc.

Rnd 5: (Slip st, ch 1, sc) in first ch-3 sp, 5 dc in next ch-3 sp, (sc in next ch-3 sp, 5 dc in next ch-3 sp) around; join with slip st to first sc, finish off.

Design by Norma Cunningham.

DAINTY FLOWERS

Continued from page 35.

ASSEMBLY

With White, using Placement Diagram as a guide, and working through **both** loops, whipstitch Blocks together forming 4 vertical strips of 5 Blocks each *(Fig. 5a, page 2)*, beginning in center sc of first corner 3-sc group and ending in center sc of next corner 3-sc group; whipstitch strips together in same manner.

PLACEMENT DIAGRAM

A B / C D	A B / C D	A B / C D	A B / C D
A B / C D	A B / C D	A B / C D	A B / C D
A B / C D	A B / C D	A B / C D	A B / C D
A B / C D	A B / C D	A B / C D	A B / C D
A B / C D	A B / C D	A B / C D	A B / C D

EDGING

Rnd 1: With **right** side facing, join White with dc in center sc of any corner 3-sc group; dc in same st and in next 27 sc, ★ (dc in same st as joining on same Block and in same st as joining on next Block, dc in next 27 sc) across to center sc of next corner 3-sc group, (2 dc, ch 1, 2 dc) in center sc, dc in next 27 sc; repeat from ★ 2 times **more**, (dc in same st as joining on same Block and in same st as joining on next Block, dc in next 27 sc) across, 2 dc in same st as first dc, sc in first dc to form last ch-1 sp: 530 dc and 4 ch-1 sps.

Rnd 2: Ch 3, (dc, ch 1, 2 dc) in last ch-1 sp made, ★ dc in each dc across to next corner ch-1 sp, (2 dc, ch 2, 2 dc) in corner ch-1 sp; repeat from ★ 2 times **more**, dc in each dc across; join with slip st to first dc, finish off: 546 dc and 4 ch-1 sps.

Rnd 3: With **right** side facing, join Yellow with sc in any corner ch-1 sp; 2 sc in same sp, sc in each dc around working 3 sc in each corner ch-1 sp; join with slip st to first sc, finish off.

Rnd 4: With **right** side facing, join Green with sc in center sc of any corner 3-sc group; 2 sc in same st, sc in next sc and in each sc around working 3 sc in center sc of each corner 3-sc group; join with slip st to first sc, finish off.

Rnd 5: With Pink, repeat Rnd 4.

Rnd 6: With Blue, repeat Rnd 4.

Design by Janice E. Smith.

SUNSHINE

Finished Size: 34" x 43"

MATERIALS
Baby Fingering Weight Yarn:
   Yellow - 9½ ounces, (270 grams, 1,465 yards)
   White - 4½ ounces, (130 grams, 695 yards)
Crochet hook, size D (3.25 mm) **or** size needed
   for gauge
Tapestry needle

GAUGE: Each Square = 4½"

Gauge Swatch: 2¼" (straight edge to straight edge)
Work same as Square Center.

STITCH GUIDE

TREBLE CROCHET *(abbreviated tr)*
YO twice, insert hook in sp indicated, YO and pull up
a loop (4 loops on hook), (YO and draw through
2 loops on hook) 3 times.

FRONT POST DOUBLE CROCHET
   (abbreviated FPdc)
YO, insert hook from **front** to **back** around post of
dc indicated *(Fig. 11)*, YO and pull up a loop even
with loop on hook (3 loops on hook), (YO and draw
through 2 loops on hook) twice.

Fig. 11

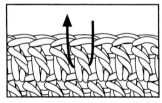

FRONT POST DOUBLE TREBLE CROCHET
   (abbreviated FPdtr)
YO 3 times, insert hook **front** to **back** around post
of sc indicated *(Fig. 11)*, YO and pull up a loop
(5 loops on hook), (YO and draw through 2 loops on
hook) 4 times.

ANCHORED DC
YO, working in **front** of Rnd 4, insert hook from **top**
to **bottom** in free loop of next dc one rnd **below**,
rotate hook ½ turn clockwise, insert hook in Back
Loop Only of next dc on Rnd 4 *(Fig. 12)*, YO and
draw through 2 sts on hook, (YO and draw through
2 loops on hook) twice **(counts as one dc)**.

Fig. 12

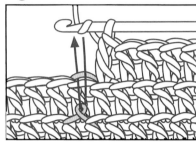

PICOT
Ch 3, slip st in third ch from hook.

SQUARE (Make 63)
CENTER BLOCK
With White, ch 5 **loosely**.

Rows 1-3 are each worked in 2 steps, working to the **left**
picking up loops and then working to the **right**
completing each stitch.

Row 1 (Right side)**:** Working from **right** to **left** and in
back ridge of beginning chs *(Fig. 1, page 1)*, insert hook
in second ch from hook, YO and pull up a loop (2 loops
on hook), pull up a loop in next 3 chs *(Fig. 13a)* (5 loops
on hook); working from **left** to **right**, YO and draw
through first loop on hook, ★ YO and draw through
2 loops on hook *(Fig. 13b)*; repeat from ★ 3 times
more. One loop remains on hook. This is the first stitch
of the next row.

Fig. 13a

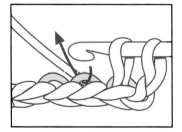

Fig. 13b

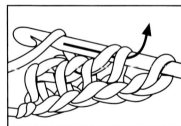

Note: Loop a short piece of yarn around any stitch on
Row 1 of Center Block only to mark **right** side.

Continued on page 43

Rows 2 and 3: Working from **right** to **left**, skip first vertical strand, ★ insert hook under next vertical strand **(Fig. 14)**, YO and pull up a loop; repeat from ★ across (5 loops on hook); working from **left** to **right**, YO and draw through first loop on hook, (YO and draw through 2 loops on hook) across.

Fig. 14

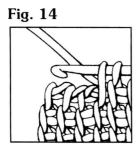

Row 4: Ch 1, working from **right** to **left**, skip first vertical strand, ★ insert hook under next vertical strand, YO and draw **loosely** through strand **and** loop on hook **(Fig. 15)**; repeat from ★ across; do **not** finish off.

Fig. 15

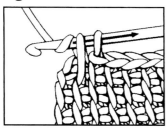

NEXT 3 BLOCKS
Work same as Center Block.

With **right** side of Center Block facing, join with slip st in next corner on Center Block; do **not** finish off.

LAST BLOCK
Work same as Center Block.

With **right** side of Center Block facing, join with slip st in next corner sp between Center Block and second Block; finish off.

BORDER

Rnd 1: With **right** side facing, join Yellow with sc in corner ch at beginning of Row 4 on Last Block **(see Joining With Sc, page 1)**; ch 3, dc in next joining slip st on Center Block, ch 3, sc in next corner ch on next Block, ch 5, ★ sc in next corner ch on same Block, ch 3, dc in next joining slip st on Center Block, ch 3, sc in next corner ch on next Block, ch 5; repeat from ★ 2 times **more**; join with slip st to first sc: 12 sts and 12 sps.

Rnd 2: Ch 1, sc in same st, (3 sc in next ch-3 sp, sc in next st) twice, (2 sc, ch 3, 2 sc) in next corner ch-5 sp, ★ sc in next sc, (3 sc in next ch-3 sp, sc in next st) twice, (2 sc, ch 3, 2 sc) in next corner ch-5 sp; repeat from ★ 2 times **more**; join with slip st to first sc, finish off: 52 sc and 4 ch-3 sps.

Rnd 3: With **right** side facing, join White with dc in any corner ch-3 sp **(see Joining With Dc, page 1)**; (dc, ch 2, 2 dc) in same sp, ★ dc in each sc across to next corner ch-3 sp, (2 dc, ch 2, 2 dc) in corner ch-3 sp; repeat from ★ 2 times **more**, dc in each sc across; join with slip st to Back Loop Only of first dc **(Fig. 2, page 1)**, finish off: 68 dc and 4 ch-2 sps.

Rnd 4: With **right** side facing, join Yellow with dc in any corner ch-2 sp; dc in same sp, ★ † dc in Back Loop Only of next 4 dc, work FPdtr around sc on Rnd 1, skip next sc from last sc made on Rnd 3, dc in Back Loop Only of next 3 dc, work FPdc around next dc, dc in Back Loop Only of next 3 dc, work FPdtr around next sc on Rnd 1, skip next sc from last sc made on Rnd 3, dc in Back Loop Only of next 4 dc †, (2 dc, ch 2, 2 dc) in next corner ch-2 sp; repeat from ★ 2 times **more**, then repeat from † to † once, 2 dc in same sp as first dc, ch 1, sc in Back Loop Only of first dc to form last ch-2 sp; do **not** finish off: 84 sts and 4 ch-2 sps.

Rnd 5: Ch 3, dc in last ch-2 sp made, ★ † dc in Back Loop Only of next 4 dc, work Anchored dc, (dc in Back Loop Only of next 3 sts, work Anchored dc) 3 times, dc in Back Loop Only of next 4 dc †, (2 dc, ch 2, 2 dc) in next corner ch-2 sp; repeat from ★ 2 times **more**, then repeat from † to † once, 2 dc in same sp as first dc, ch 2, join with slip st to first dc, finish off: 100 sts and 4 ch-2 sps.

CENTER TRIM

Rnd 1: With **right** side facing, keeping yarn to front, and working in end of rows along inside edge of outer Blocks, join Yellow with slip st in first row of any outer Block; slip st in next 2 rows, (slip st in next 3 rows on next Block) 3 times; do **not** join: 12 slip sts.

Rnd 2: Slip st in next 12 slip sts; join with slip st to next slip st, finish off.

ASSEMBLY

With Yellow, using Placement Diagram as a guide, and working through **inside** loops only, whipstitch Squares together forming 7 vertical strips of 9 Squares each *(Fig. 5b, page 2)*, beginning in second ch of first corner ch-2 and ending in first ch of next corner ch-2; whipstitch strips together in same manner.

PLACEMENT DIAGRAM

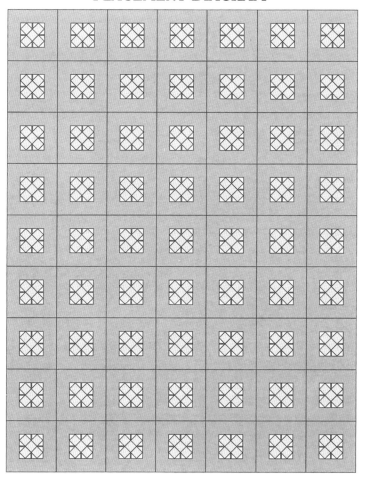

EDGING

Rnd 1: With **right** side facing, join Yellow with sc in any corner ch-2 sp; working in both loops, sc in each dc and in each unworked ch across to next corner ch-2 sp, ★ 3 sc in corner ch-2 sp, sc in each dc and in each unworked ch across to next corner ch-2 sp; repeat from ★ 2 times **more**, 2 sc in same sp as first sc; join with slip st to first sc, finish off: 868 sc.

Rnd 2: With **right** side facing, join White with dc in third sc of any corner 3-sc group; dc in same st, ★ † work Picot, skip next sc, 2 dc in next sc, work Picot, (skip next 2 sc, 2 dc in next sc, work Picot) across to center sc of next corner 3-sc group, skip center sc †, 2 dc in next sc; repeat from ★ 2 times **more**, then repeat from † to † once; join with slip st to first dc, finish off: 292 2-dc groups.

Rnd 3: With **right** side facing, skip first dc of any 2-dc group and join Yellow with slip st in sp **before** next dc; ch 4, tr in same sp, work Picot, ★ skip next Picot and next dc, 2 tr in sp **before** next dc, work Picot; repeat from ★ around; join with slip st to top of beginning ch-4, finish off.

Design by Mary C. Abadir.

GUARDIAN ANGEL

Finished Size: 39½" x 34½"

MATERIALS
Worsted Weight Yarn:
  24 ounces, (680 grams, 1,575 yards)
Crochet hook, size G (4.00 mm) **or** size needed
  for gauge

GAUGE: In pattern, 15 sts and 17 rows = 4"

Gauge Swatch: 4" square
Ch 16 **loosely**.
Row 1: Sc in second ch from hook and in each ch
across: 15 sc.
Rows 2-17: Ch 1, turn; sc in each sc across.
Finish off.

STITCH GUIDE

LOOP STITCH (*abbreviated Loop St*)
Insert hook in next st, wrap yarn around index finger
of left hand once **more**, insert hook through both
strands on finger following direction indicated by
arrow **(Fig. 16a)**, being careful to hook both strands
(Fig. 16b), draw through st pulling loop to measure
approximately ¾", remove finger from loop, YO and
draw through all 3 loops on hook **(Loop St made,
Fig. 16c)**.

Fig. 16a

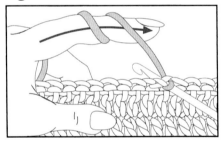

Fig. 16b

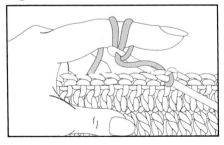

Fig. 16c

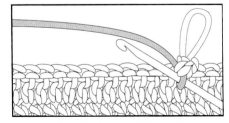

CHAIN LOOP (*abbreviated Ch Loop*)
Insert hook in next sc, YO and pull up a loop, (YO
and draw through one loop on hook) 3 times, YO
and draw through both loops on hook.

AFGHAN BODY
Ch 146 **loosely**.

Row 1 (Right side)**:** Sc in second ch from hook and in
each ch across: 145 sc.

Rows 2-5: Ch 1, turn; sc in each sc across.

Row 6: Ch 1, turn; sc in first 47 sc, (work 2 Loop Sts,
sc in next 47 sc) twice: 141 sc and 4 Loop Sts.

Row 7: Ch 1, turn; sc in each st across: 145 sc.

Row 8: Ch 1, turn; sc in first 45 sc, work 4 Loop Sts,
sc in next 47 sc, work 4 Loop Sts, sc in last 45 sc:
137 sc and 8 Loop Sts.

Row 9: Ch 1, turn; sc in each st across: 145 sc.

Row 10: Ch 1, turn; sc in first 43 sc, work 5 Loop Sts,
sc in next 49 sc, work 5 Loop Sts, sc in last 43 sc:
135 sc and 10 Loop Sts.

Row 11: Ch 1, turn; sc in each st across: 145 sc.

Row 12: Ch 1, turn; sc in first 42 sc, work 5 Loop Sts,
sc in next 51 sc, work 5 Loop Sts, sc in last 42 sc:
135 sc and 10 Loop Sts.

Row 13: Ch 1, turn; sc in each st across: 145 sc.

Row 14: Ch 1, turn; sc in first 40 sc, work 6 Loop Sts,
sc in next 2 sc, work 2 Loop Sts, sc in next 45 sc, work
2 Loop Sts, sc in next 2 sc, work 6 Loop Sts, sc in last
40 sc: 129 sc and 16 Loop Sts.

Row 15: Ch 1, turn; sc in first 57 sts, work Ch Loop,
(sc in next sc, work Ch Loop) 6 times, sc in next 5 sc,
work Ch Loop, (sc in next sc, work Ch Loop) 6 times, sc
in last 57 sts: 131 sc and 14 Ch Loops.

Row 16: Ch 1, turn; sc in first 39 sc, work 6 Loop Sts,
sc in next sc, work 4 Loop Sts, sc in next 45 sts, work
4 Loop Sts, sc in next sc, work 6 Loop Sts, sc in last
39 sc: 125 sc and 20 Loop Sts.

Row 17: Ch 1, turn; sc in first 54 sts, work Ch Loop,
(sc in next sc, work Ch Loop) 18 times, sc in last 54 sts:
126 sc and 19 Ch Loops.

Row 18: Ch 1, turn; sc in first 38 sc, work 5 Loop Sts,
sc in next sc, work 4 Loop Sts, sc in next 49 sts, work
4 Loop Sts, sc in next sc, work 5 Loop Sts, sc in last
38 sc: 127 sc and 18 Loop Sts.

Row 19: Ch 1, turn; sc in first 12 sc, work Ch Loop, sc
in next 38 sts, work Ch Loop, (sc in next sc, work
Ch Loop) 21 times, sc in next 38 sts, work Ch Loop, sc
in last 12 sc; do **not** finish off: 121 sc and 24 Ch Loops.

Continued on page 47.

Row 20: Ch 1, turn; sc in first 37 sts, work 5 Loop Sts, sc in next 2 sc, work 3 Loop Sts, sc in next 51 sts, work 3 Loop Sts, sc in next 2 sc, work 5 Loop Sts, sc in last 37 sts: 129 sc and 16 Loop Sts.

Row 21: Ch 1, turn; sc in first 11 sc, work Ch Loop, sc in next sc, work Ch Loop, sc in next 36 sts, work Ch Loop, (sc in next sc, work Ch Loop) 22 times, sc in next 36 sts, work Ch Loop, sc in next sc, work Ch Loop, sc in last 11 sc: 118 sc and 27 Ch Loops.

Row 22: Ch 1, turn; sc in first 36 sts, work 10 Loop Sts, sc in next 53 sts, work 10 Loop Sts, sc in last 36 sts: 125 sc and 20 Loop Sts.

Row 23: Ch 1, turn; sc in first 10 sc, work Ch Loop, (sc in next sc, work Ch Loop) twice, sc in next 34 sts, work Ch Loop, (sc in next sc, work Ch Loop) 23 times, sc in next 34 sts, work Ch Loop, (sc in next sc, work Ch Loop) twice, sc in last 10 sc: 115 sc and 30 Ch Loops.

Row 24: Ch 1, turn; sc in first 35 sts, work 10 Loop Sts, sc in next 55 sts, work 10 Loop Sts, sc in last 35 sts: 125 sc and 20 Loop Sts.

Row 25: Ch 1, turn; sc in first 9 sc, work Ch Loop, (sc in next sc, work Ch Loop) 3 times, sc in next 34 sts, work Ch Loop, (sc in next sc, work Ch Loop) 22 times, sc in next 34 sts, work Ch Loop, (sc in next sc, work Ch Loop) 3 times, sc in last 9 sc: 114 sc and 31 Ch Loops.

Row 26: Ch 1, turn; sc in first 34 sts, work 10 Loop Sts, sc in next 57 sts, work 10 Loop Sts, sc in last 34 sts: 125 sc and 20 Loop Sts.

Row 27: Ch 1, turn; sc in first 8 sc, work Ch Loop, (sc in next sc, work Ch Loop) 4 times, sc in next 36 sts, work Ch Loop, (sc in next sc, work Ch Loop) 19 times, sc in next 36 sts, work Ch Loop, (sc in next sc, work Ch Loop) 4 times, sc in last 8 sc: 115 sc and 30 Ch Loops.

Row 28: Ch 1, turn; sc in first 33 sts, work 10 Loop Sts, sc in next 59 sts, work 10 Loop Sts, sc in last 33 sts: 125 sc and 20 Loop Sts.

Row 29: Ch 1, turn; sc in first 7 sc, work Ch Loop, (sc in next sc, work Ch Loop) 5 times, sc in next 38 sts, work Ch Loop, (sc in next sc, work Ch Loop) 16 times, sc in next 38 sts, work Ch Loop, (sc in next sc, work Ch Loop) 5 times, sc in last 7 sc: 116 sc and 29 Ch Loops.

Row 30: Ch 1, turn; sc in first 32 sts, work 10 Loop Sts, sc in next 3 sc, work 3 Loop Sts, sc in next 49 sts, work 3 Loop Sts, sc in next 3 sc, work 10 Loop Sts, sc in last 32 sts: 119 sc and 26 Loop Sts.

Row 31: Ch 1, turn; sc in first 6 sc, work Ch Loop, (sc in next sc, work Ch Loop) 6 times, sc in next 38 sts, work Ch Loop, (sc in next sc, work Ch Loop) 15 times, sc in next 38 sts, work Ch Loop, (sc in next sc, work Ch Loop) 6 times, sc in last 6 sc: 115 sc and 30 Ch Loops.

Row 32: Ch 1, turn; sc in first 31 sts, work 11 Loop Sts, sc in next sc, work 5 Loop Sts, sc in next 49 sts, work 5 Loop Sts, sc in next sc, work 11 Loop Sts, sc in last 31 sts: 113 sc and 32 Loop Sts.

Row 33: Ch 1, turn; sc in first 6 sc, work Ch Loop, (sc in next sc, work Ch Loop) twice, sc in next 3 sc, work Ch Loop, (sc in next sc, work Ch Loop) twice, sc in next 37 sts, work Ch Loop, (sc in next sc, work Ch Loop) 16 times, sc in next 37 sts, work Ch Loop, (sc in next sc, work Ch Loop) twice, sc in next 3 sc, work Ch Loop, (sc in next sc, work Ch Loop) twice, sc in last 6 sc: 116 sc and 29 Ch Loops.

Row 34: Ch 1, turn; sc in first 30 sts, work 16 Loop Sts, sc in next 53 sts, work 16 Loop Sts, sc in last 30 sts: 113 sc and 32 Loop Sts.

Row 35: Ch 1, turn; sc in first 7 sc, work Ch Loop, sc in next sc, work Ch Loop, sc in next 5 sc, work Ch Loop, sc in next sc, work Ch Loop, sc in next 39 sts, work Ch Loop, (sc in next sc, work Ch Loop) 15 times, sc in next 39 sts, work Ch Loop, sc in next sc, work Ch Loop, sc in next 5 sc, work Ch Loop, sc in next sc, work Ch Loop, sc in last 7 sc: 121 sc and 24 Ch Loops.

Row 36: Ch 1, turn; sc in first 30 sts, work 15 Loop Sts, sc in next 55 sts, work 15 Loop Sts, sc in last 30 sts: 115 sc and 30 Loop Sts.

Row 37: Ch 1, turn; sc in first 56 sts, work Ch Loop, (sc in next sc, work Ch Loop) 16 times, sc in last 56 sts: 128 sc and 17 Ch Loops.

Row 38: Ch 1, turn; sc in first 29 sc, work 15 Loop Sts, sc in next 57 sts, work 15 Loop Sts, sc in last 29 sc: 115 sc and 30 Loop Sts.

Row 39: Ch 1, turn; sc in first 57 sts, work Ch Loop, (sc in next sc, work Ch Loop) 15 times, sc in last 57 sts: 129 sc and 16 Ch Loops.

Row 40: Ch 1, turn; sc in first 29 sc, work 14 Loop Sts, sc in next 59 sts, work 14 Loop Sts, sc in last 29 sc: 117 sc and 28 Loop Sts.

Row 41: Repeat Row 37.

Row 42: Ch 1, turn; sc in first 28 sc, work 14 Loop Sts, sc in next 61 sts, work 14 Loop Sts, sc in last 28 sc: 117 sc and 28 Loop Sts.

Row 43: Repeat Row 39.

Row 44: Repeat Row 42.

Row 45: Repeat Row 37.

Row 46: Ch 1, turn; sc in first 27 sc, work 14 Loop Sts, sc in next 63 sts, work 14 Loop Sts, sc in last 27 sc: 117 sc and 28 Loop Sts.

Row 47: Repeat Row 39.

Row 48: Repeat Row 46.

Row 49: Ch 1, turn; sc in first 58 sts, work Ch Loop, (sc in next sc, work Ch Loop) 14 times, sc in last 58 sts: 130 sc and 15 Ch Loops.

Row 50: Ch 1, turn; sc in first 26 sc, work 15 Loop Sts, sc in next 63 sts, work 15 Loop Sts, sc in last 26 sc: 115 sc and 30 Loop Sts.

Row 51: Repeat Row 39.

Row 52: Ch 1, turn; sc in first 26 sc, work 14 Loop Sts, sc in next 2 sc, work 2 Loop Sts, sc in next 57 sts, work 2 Loop Sts, sc in next 2 sc, work 14 Loop Sts, sc in last 26 sc: 113 sc and 32 Loop Sts.

Row 53: Repeat Row 49.

Row 54: Ch 1, turn; sc in first 26 sc, work 18 Loop Sts, sc in next 57 sts, work 18 Loop Sts, sc in last 26 sc: 109 sc and 36 Loop Sts.

Row 55: Repeat Row 39.

Row 56: Repeat Row 54.

Row 57: Repeat Row 49.

Row 58: Ch 1, turn; sc in first 26 sc, work 17 Loop Sts, sc in next 59 sts, work 17 Loop Sts, sc in last 26 sc: 111 sc and 34 Loop Sts.

Row 59: Repeat Row 39.

Row 60: Ch 1, turn; sc in first 25 sc, work 17 Loop Sts, sc in next 2 sc, work Loop St, sc in next 55 sts, work Loop St, sc in next 2 sc, work 17 Loop Sts, sc in last 25 sc: 109 sc and 36 Loop Sts.

Row 61: Repeat Row 49.

Row 62: Ch 1, turn; sc in first 25 sc, work 17 Loop Sts, sc in next sc, work 2 Loop Sts, sc in next 55 sts, work 2 Loop Sts, sc in next sc, work 17 Loop Sts, sc in last 25 sc: 107 sc and 38 Loop Sts.

Row 63: Ch 1, turn; sc in first 12 sc, work Ch Loop, sc in next 44 sts, work Ch Loop, (sc in next sc, work Ch Loop) 15 times, sc in next 44 sts, work Ch Loop, sc in last 12 sc: 127 sc and 18 Ch Loops.

Row 64: Ch 1, turn; sc in first 25 sts, work 20 Loop Sts, sc in next 10 sc, work 2 Loop Sts, sc in next 31 sts, work 2 Loop Sts, sc in next 10 sc, work 20 Loop Sts, sc in last 25 sts: 101 sc and 44 Loop Sts.

Row 65: Ch 1, turn; sc in first 11 sc, work Ch Loop, sc in next sc, work Ch Loop, sc in next 44 sts, work Ch Loop, (sc in next sc, work Ch Loop) 14 times, sc in next 44 sts, work Ch Loop, sc in next sc, work Ch Loop, sc in last 11 sc: 126 sc and 19 Ch Loops.

Row 66: Ch 1, turn; sc in first 25 sts, work 20 Loop Sts, sc in next 8 sc, work 4 Loop Sts, sc in next 31 sts, work 4 Loop Sts, sc in next 8 sc, work 20 Loop Sts, sc in last 25 sts: 97 sc and 48 Loop Sts.

Row 67: Ch 1, turn; sc in first 10 sc, work Ch Loop, (sc in next sc, work Ch Loop) twice, sc in next 42 sts, work Ch Loop, (sc in next sc, work Ch Loop) 15 times, sc in next 42 sts, work Ch Loop, (sc in next sc, work Ch Loop) twice, sc in last 10 sc: 123 sc and 22 Ch Loops.

Row 68: Ch 1, turn; sc in first 25 sts, work 20 Loop Sts, sc in next sc, work Loop St, sc in next 5 sc, work 5 Loop Sts, sc in next 31 sts, work 5 Loop Sts, sc in next 5 sc, work Loop St, sc in next sc, work 20 Loop Sts, sc in last 25 sts: 93 sc and 52 Loop Sts.

Row 69: Ch 1, turn; sc in first 9 sc, work Ch Loop, (sc in next sc, work Ch Loop) 3 times, sc in next 42 sts, work Ch Loop, (sc in next sc, work Ch Loop) 14 times, sc in next 42 sts, work Ch Loop, (sc in next sc, work Ch Loop) 3 times, sc in last 9 sc: 122 sc and 23 Ch Loops.

Row 70: Ch 1, turn; sc in first 25 sts, work 22 Loop Sts, sc in next 4 sc, work 6 Loop Sts, sc in next 31 sts, work 6 Loop Sts, sc in next 4 sc, work 22 Loop Sts, sc in last 25 sts: 89 sc and 56 Loop Sts.

Row 71: Ch 1, turn; sc in first 8 sc, work Ch Loop, (sc in next sc, work Ch Loop) 4 times, sc in next 40 sts, work Ch Loop, (sc in next sc, work Ch Loop) 15 times, sc in next 40 sts, work Ch Loop, (sc in next sc, work Ch Loop) 4 times, sc in last 8 sc: 119 sc and 26 Ch Loops.

Row 72: Ch 1, turn; sc in first 25 sts, work 23 Loop Sts, sc in next sc, work Loop St, sc in next sc, work 5 Loop Sts, sc in next 33 sts, work 5 Loop Sts, sc in next sc, work Loop St, sc in next sc, work 23 Loop Sts, sc in last 25 sts: 87 sc and 58 Loop Sts.

Row 73: Ch 1, turn; sc in first 7 sc, work Ch Loop, (sc in next sc, work Ch Loop) 5 times, sc in next 38 sts, work Ch Loop, (sc in next sc, work Ch Loop) 16 times, sc in next 38 sts, work Ch Loop, (sc in next sc, work Ch Loop) 5 times, sc in last 7 sc: 116 sc and 29 Ch Loops.

Row 74: Ch 1, turn; sc in first 25 sts, work 30 Loop Sts, sc in next 35 sts, work 30 Loop Sts, sc in last 25 sts: 85 sc and 60 Loop Sts.

Row 75: Ch 1, turn; sc in first 6 sc, work Ch Loop, (sc in next sc, work Ch Loop) 6 times, sc in next 36 sts, work Ch Loop, (sc in next sc, work Ch Loop) 17 times, sc in next 36 sts, work Ch Loop, (sc in next sc, work Ch Loop) 6 times, sc in last 6 sc: 113 sc and 32 Ch Loops.

Row 76: Repeat Row 74.

Row 77: Ch 1, turn; sc in first 6 sc, work Ch Loop, (sc in next sc, work Ch Loop) twice, sc in next 3 sc, work Ch Loop, (sc in next sc, work Ch Loop) twice, sc in next 37 sts, work Ch Loop, (sc in next sc, work Ch Loop) 16 times, sc in next 37 sts, work Ch Loop, (sc in next sc, work Ch Loop) twice, sc in next 3 sc, work Ch Loop, (sc in next sc, work Ch Loop) twice, sc in last 6 sc: 116 sc and 29 Ch Loops.

Row 78: Repeat Row 74.

Row 79: Ch 1, turn; sc in first 7 sc, work Ch Loop, sc in next sc, work Ch Loop, sc in next 5 sc, work Ch Loop, sc in next sc, work Ch Loop, sc in next 37 sts, work Ch Loop, (sc in next sc, work Ch Loop) 17 times, sc in next 37 sts, work Ch Loop, sc in next sc, work Ch Loop, sc in next 5 sc, work Ch Loop, sc in next sc, work Ch Loop, sc in last 7 sc: 119 sc and 26 Ch Loops.

Row 80: Repeat Row 74.

Row 81: Ch 1, turn; sc in first 56 sts, work Ch Loop, (sc in next sc, work Ch Loop) 16 times, sc in last 56 sts; do **not** finish off: 128 sc and 17 Ch Loops.

Continued on page 49.

Row 82: Ch 1, turn; sc in first 26 sc, work 29 Loop Sts, sc in next 35 sts, work 29 Loop Sts, sc in last 26 sc: 87 sc and 58 Loop Sts.

Row 83: Ch 1, turn; sc in first 55 sts, work Ch Loop, (sc in next sc, work Ch Loop) 17 times, sc in last 55 sts: 127 sc and 18 Ch Loops.

Row 84: Repeat Row 82.

Rows 85-87: Repeat Rows 81-83.

Row 88: Ch 1, turn; sc in first 26 sc, work 30 Loop Sts, sc in next 33 sts, work 30 Loop Sts, sc in last 26 sc: 85 sc and 60 Loop Sts.

Row 89: Repeat Row 81.

Row 90: Ch 1, turn; sc in first 27 sc, work 29 Loop Sts, sc in next 33 sts, work 29 Loop Sts, sc in last 27 sc: 87 sc and 58 Loop Sts.

Row 91: Ch 1, turn; sc in first 57 sts, work Ch Loop, (sc in next sc, work Ch Loop) 15 times, sc in last 57 sts: 129 sc and 16 Ch Loops.

Row 92: Repeat Row 90.

Row 93: Repeat Row 81.

Rows 94 and 95: Repeat Rows 90 and 91.

Row 96: Ch 1, turn; sc in first 28 sc, work 28 Loop Sts, sc in next 33 sts, work 28 Loop Sts, sc in last 28 sc: 89 sc and 56 Loop Sts.

Row 97: Repeat Row 81.

Row 98: Ch 1, turn; sc in first 29 sc, work 28 Loop Sts, sc in next 31 sts, work 28 Loop Sts, sc in last 29 sc: 89 sc and 56 Loop Sts.

Row 99: Repeat Row 91.

Row 100: Ch 1, turn; sc in first 29 sc, (work 29 Loop Sts, sc in next 29 sts) twice: 87 sc and 58 Loop Sts.

Row 101: Ch 1, turn; sc in first 58 sts, work Ch Loop, (sc in next sc, work Ch Loop) 14 times, sc in last 58 sts: 130 sc and 15 Ch Loops.

Row 102: Ch 1, turn; sc in first 30 sc, work 29 Loop Sts, sc in next 27 sts, work 29 Loop Sts, sc in last 30 sc: 87 sc and 58 Loop Sts.

Row 103: Ch 1, turn; sc in first 59 sts, work Ch Loop, (sc in next sc, work Ch Loop) 13 times, sc in last 59 sts: 131 sc and 14 Ch Loops.

Row 104: Ch 1, turn; sc in first 31 sc, work 29 Loop Sts, sc in next 25 sts, work 29 Loop Sts, sc in last 31 sc: 87 sc and 58 Loop Sts.

Row 105: Ch 1, turn; sc in first 60 sts, work Ch Loop, (sc in next sc, work Ch Loop) 12 times, sc in last 60 sts: 132 sc and 13 Ch Loops.

Row 106: Ch 1, turn; sc in first 32 sc, work 29 Loop Sts, sc in next 23 sts, work 29 Loop Sts, sc in last 32 sc: 87 sc and 58 Loop Sts.

Row 107: Ch 1, turn; sc in first 12 sc, work Ch Loop, sc in next 48 sts, work Ch Loop, (sc in next sc, work Ch Loop) 11 times, sc in next 48 sts, work Ch Loop, sc in last 12 sc: 131 sc and 14 Ch Loops.

Row 108: Ch 1, turn; sc in first 32 sts, work 32 Loop Sts, sc in next 17 sts, work 32 Loop Sts, sc in last 32 sts: 81 sc and 64 Loop Sts.

Row 109: Ch 1, turn; sc in first 11 sc, work Ch Loop, sc in next sc, work Ch Loop, sc in next 50 sts, work Ch Loop, (sc in next sc, work Ch Loop) 8 times, sc in next 50 sts, work Ch Loop, sc in next sc, work Ch Loop sc in last 11 sc: 132 sc and 13 Ch Loops.

Row 110: Ch 1, turn; sc in first 33 sts, work 31 Loop Sts, sc in next 17 sts, work 31 Loop Sts, sc in last 33 sts: 83 sc and 62 Loop Sts.

Row 111: Ch 1, turn; sc in first 10 sc, work Ch Loop, (sc in next sc, work Ch Loop) twice, sc in next 52 sts, work Ch Loop, (sc in next sc, work Ch Loop) 5 times, sc in next 52 sts, work Ch Loop, (sc in next sc, work Ch Loop) twice, sc in last 10 sc: 133 sc and 12 Ch Loops.

Row 112: Ch 1, turn; sc in first 34 sts, work 29 Loop Sts, sc in next 19 sts, work 29 Loop Sts, sc in last 34 sts: 87 sc and 58 Loop Sts.

Row 113: Ch 1, turn; sc in first 9 sc, work Ch Loop, (sc in next sc, work Ch Loop) 3 times, sc in next 50 sts, work Ch Loop, (sc in next sc, work Ch Loop) 6 times, sc in next 50 sts, work Ch Loop, (sc in next sc, work Ch Loop) 3 times, sc in last 9 sc: 130 sc and 15 Ch Loops.

Row 114: Ch 1, turn; sc in first 35 sts, work 27 Loop Sts, sc in next 21 sts, work 27 Loop Sts, sc in last 35 sts: 91 sc and 54 Loop Sts.

Row 115: Ch 1, turn; sc in first 8 sc, work Ch Loop, (sc in next sc, work Ch Loop) 4 times, sc in next 48 sts, work Ch Loop, (sc in next sc, work Ch Loop) 7 times, sc in next 48 sts, work Ch Loop, (sc in next sc, work Ch Loop) 4 times, sc in last 8 sc: 127 sc and 18 Ch Loops.

Row 116: Ch 1, turn; sc in first 36 sts, work 25 Loop Sts, sc in next 23 sts, work 25 Loop Sts, sc in last 36 sts: 95 sc and 50 Loop Sts.

Row 117: Ch 1, turn; sc in first 7 sc, work Ch Loop, (sc in next sc, work Ch Loop) 5 times, sc in next 45 sts, work Ch Loop, sc in next 2 sc, work Ch Loop, (sc in next sc, work Ch Loop) 6 times, sc in next 2 sc, work Ch Loop, sc in next 45 sts, work Ch Loop, (sc in next sc work Ch Loop) 5 times, sc in last 7 sc: 124 sc and 21 Ch Loops.

Row 118: Ch 1, turn; sc in first 37 sts, work 24 Loop Sts, sc in next 23 sts, work 24 Loop Sts, sc in last 37 sts: 97 sc and 48 Loop Sts.

Row 119: Ch 1, turn; sc in first 6 sc, work Ch Loop, (sc in next sc, work Ch Loop) 6 times, sc in next 44 sts, work Ch Loop, sc in next 2 sc, work Ch Loop, (sc in next sc, work Ch Loop) 6 times, sc in next 2 sc, work Ch Loop, sc in next 44 sts, work Ch Loop, (sc in next sc, work Ch Loop) 6 times, sc in last 6 sc: 122 sc and 23 Ch Loops.

Row 120: Ch 1, turn; sc in first 38 sts, work 23 Loop Sts, sc in next 23 sts, work 23 Loop Sts, sc in last 38 sts: 99 sc and 46 Loop Sts.

Row 121: Ch 1, turn; sc in first 6 sc, work Ch Loop, (sc in next sc, work Ch Loop) twice, sc in next 3 sc, work Ch Loop, (sc in next sc, work Ch Loop) twice, sc in next 44 sts, work Ch Loop, sc in next 2 sc, work Ch Loop, (sc in next sc, work Ch Loop) 6 times, sc in next 2 sc, work Ch Loop, sc in next 44 sts, work Ch Loop, (sc in next sc, work Ch Loop) twice, sc in next 3 sc, work Ch Loop, (sc in next sc, work Ch Loop) twice, sc in last 6 sc: 124 sc and 21 Ch Loops.

Row 122: Ch 1, turn; sc in first 39 sts, work 22 Loop Sts, sc in next 23 sts, work 22 Loop Sts, sc in last 39 sts: 101 sc and 44 Loop Sts.

Row 123: Ch 1, turn; sc in first 7 sc, work Ch Loop, sc in next sc, work Ch Loop, sc in next 5 sc, work Ch Loop, sc in next sc, work Ch Loop, sc in next 45 sts, work Ch Loop, sc in next 2 sc, work Ch Loop, (sc in next sc, work Ch Loop) 6 times, sc in next 2 sc, work Ch Loop, sc in next 45 sts, work Ch Loop, sc in next sc, work Ch Loop, sc in next 5 sc, work Ch Loop, sc in next sc, work Ch Loop, sc in last 7 sc: 128 sc and 17 Ch Loops.

Row 124: Ch 1, turn; sc in first 41 sts, work 21 Loop Sts, sc in next 21 sts, work 21 Loop Sts, sc in last 41 sts: 103 sc and 42 Loop Sts.

Row 125: Ch 1, turn; sc in first 63 sts, work Ch Loop, sc in next 4 sc, work Ch Loop, (sc in next sc, work Ch Loop) 4 times, sc in next 4 sc, work Ch Loop, sc in last 63 sts: 138 sc and 7 Ch Loops.

Row 126: Ch 1, turn; sc in first 43 sc, work 19 Loop Sts, sc in next 21 sts, work 19 Loop Sts, sc in last 43 sc: 107 sc and 38 Loop Sts.

Row 127: Ch 1, turn; sc in first 65 sts, work Ch Loop, sc in next 13 sc, work Ch Loop, sc in last 65 sts: 143 sc and 2 Ch Loops.

Row 128: Ch 1, turn; sc in first 45 sc, work 18 Loop Sts, sc in next 19 sts, work 18 Loop Sts, sc in last 45 sc: 109 sc and 36 Loop Sts.

Row 129: Ch 1, turn; sc in first 67 sts, work Ch Loop, (sc in next sc, work Ch Loop) 5 times, sc in last 67 sts: 139 sc and 6 Ch Loops.

Row 130: Ch 1, turn; sc in first 47 sc, work 16 Loop Sts, sc in next 19 sts, work 16 Loop Sts, sc in last 47 sc: 113 sc and 32 Loop Sts.

Row 131: Ch 1, turn; sc in each st across: 145 sc.

Row 132: Ch 1, turn; sc in first 49 sc, work 15 Loop Sts, sc in next 17 sc, work 15 Loop Sts, sc in last 49 sc: 115 sc and 30 Loop Sts.

Row 133: Ch 1, turn; sc in each st across: 145 sc.

Row 134: Ch 1, turn; sc in first 51 sc, work 13 Loop Sts, sc in next 17 sc, work 13 Loop Sts, sc in last 51 sc: 119 sc and 26 Loop Sts.

Row 135: Ch 1, turn; sc in each st across: 145 sc.

Row 136: Ch 1, turn; sc in first 54 sc, work 10 Loop Sts, sc in next 17 sc, work 10 Loop Sts, sc in last 54 sc: 125 sc and 20 Loop Sts.

Row 137: Ch 1, turn; sc in each st across: 145 sc.

Row 138: Ch 1, turn; sc in first 58 sc, work 5 Loop Sts, sc in next 19 sc, work 5 Loop Sts, sc in last 58 sc: 135 sc and 10 Loop Sts.

Rows 139-143: Ch 1, turn; sc in each st across: 145 sc.

Do **not** finish off.

EDGING
Rnd 1: Ch 1, do **not** turn; 2 sc in top of last sc made; sc in end of next row and in each row across; working in free loops of beginning ch *(Fig. 3, page 1)*, 3 sc in first ch, sc in next ch and in each ch across to ch at base of last sc, 3 sc in ch at base of last sc; sc in end of each row across to last row, skip last row; working in sc across Row 143, 3 sc in first sc, sc in next sc and in each sc across, sc in same st as first sc; join with slip st to Back Loop Only of first sc *(Fig. 2, page 1)*.

Rnd 2: Ch 1, working in Back Loops Only, 3 sc in same st, sc in each sc around working 3 sc in center sc of each corner 3-sc group; join with slip st to **both** loops of first sc, finish off.

Design by Carole G. Wilder.

BABY LACE

Finished Size: 48" diameter

MATERIALS
Worsted Weight Yarn:
26 ounces, (740 grams, 1,470 yards)
Crochet hook, size H (5.00 mm) **or** size needed
for gauge

GAUGE SWATCH: 5" diameter
Work same as Afghan through Rnd 3.

STITCH GUIDE

> **TREBLE CROCHET** *(abbreviated tr)*
> YO twice, insert hook in st or sp indicated, YO and
> pull up a loop (4 loops on hook), (YO and draw
> through 2 loops on hook) 3 times.

AFGHAN

Ch 5; join with slip st to form a ring.

Rnd 1 (Right side)**:** Ch 3 **(counts as first dc, now
and throughout)**, dc in ring, (ch 2, 2 dc in ring) 7 times,
ch 1, sc in first dc to form last ch-2 sp: 8 ch-2 sps.

Rnd 2: Ch 3, dc in last ch-2 sp made, (2 dc, ch 2, 2 dc)
in next ch-2 sp and in each ch-2 sp around, 2 dc in same
sp as first dc, ch 1, sc in first dc to form last ch-2 sp.

Rnd 3: Ch 3, 2 dc in last ch-2 sp made, ch 1, ★ (3 dc,
ch 2, 3 dc) in next ch-2 sp, ch 1; repeat from ★ around,
3 dc in same sp as first dc, ch 1, sc in first dc to form last
ch-2 sp: 16 sps.

Rnd 4: Ch 3, 3 dc in last ch-2 sp made, ch 1, sc in next
ch-1 sp, ch 1, ★ (4 dc, ch 3, 4 dc) in next ch-2 sp, ch 1,
sc in next ch-1 sp, ch 1; repeat from ★ around, 4 dc in
same sp as first dc, ch 1, hdc in first dc to form last
ch-3 sp: 72 sts and 24 sps.

Rnd 5: Ch 3, 4 dc in last ch-3 sp made, ch 2, skip next
4 dc, sc in next sc, ch 2, skip next ch-1 sp, ★ (5 dc, ch 3,
5 dc) in next ch-3 sp, ch 2, skip next 4 dc, sc in next sc,
ch 2, skip next ch-1 sp; repeat from ★ around, 5 dc in
same sp as first dc, ch 1, hdc in first dc to form last
ch-3 sp: 88 sts and 24 sps.

Rnd 6: Ch 3, 4 dc in last ch-3 sp made, ch 1, tr in next
ch-2 sp, tr in next sc and in next ch-2 sp, ch 1, ★ (5 dc,
ch 3, 5 dc) in next ch-3 sp, ch 1, tr in next ch-2 sp, tr in
next sc and in next ch-2 sp, ch 1; repeat from ★ around,
5 dc in same sp as first dc, ch 1, hdc in first dc to form
last ch-3 sp: 104 sts and 24 sps.

Rnd 7: Ch 3, 4 dc in last ch-3 sp made, ch 2, tr in next
ch-1 sp, tr in next 3 tr and in next ch-1 sp, ch 2, ★ (5 dc,
ch 3, 5 dc) in next ch-3 sp, ch 2, tr in next ch-1 sp, tr in
next 3 tr and in next ch-1 sp, ch 2; repeat from ★
around, 5 dc in same sp as first dc, ch 1, hdc in first dc to
form last ch-3 sp: 120 sts and 24 sps.

Rnd 8: Ch 3, 4 dc in last ch-3 sp made, ch 1, tr in next
ch-2 sp, tr in next 5 tr and in next ch-2 sp, ch 1, ★ (5 dc,
ch 3, 5 dc) in next ch-3 sp, ch 1, tr in next ch-2 sp, tr in
next 5 tr and in next ch-2 sp, ch 1; repeat from ★
around, 5 dc in same sp as first dc, ch 1, hdc in first dc to
form last ch-3 sp: 136 sts and 24 sps.

Rnd 9: Ch 3, 4 dc in last ch-3 sp made, ch 1, tr in next
ch-1 sp and in next 2 tr, ch 3, skip next 3 tr, tr in next
2 tr and in next ch-1 sp, ch 1, ★ (5 dc, ch 3, 5 dc) in next
ch-3 sp, ch 1, tr in next ch-1 sp and in next 2 tr, ch 3,
skip next 3 tr, tr in next 2 tr and in next ch-1 sp, ch 1;
repeat from ★ around, 5 dc in same sp as first dc, ch 1,
hdc in first dc to form last ch-3 sp: 128 sts and 32 sps.

Rnd 10: Ch 3, 4 dc in last ch-3 sp made, ★ † ch 1, skip
next 5 dc, tr in next tr, dc in next tr, hdc in next tr, ch 1,
(3 dc, ch 3, 3 dc) in next ch-3 sp, ch 1, hdc in next tr, dc
in next tr, tr in next tr, ch 1, skip next ch-1 sp †, (5 dc,
ch 3, 5 dc) in next ch-3 sp; repeat from ★ 6 times **more**,
then repeat from † to † once, 5 dc in same sp as first dc,
ch 1, hdc in first dc to form last ch-3 sp: 176 sts and
48 sps.

Rnd 11: Ch 3, 4 dc in last ch-3 sp made, ★ † ch 1, tr in
next ch-1 sp, tr in next 3 sts and in next ch-1 sp, ch 1,
(4 dc, ch 3, 4 dc) in next ch-3 sp, ch 1, tr in next ch-1 sp,
tr in next 3 sts and in next ch-1 sp, ch 1 †, (5 dc, ch 3,
5 dc) in next ch-3 sp; repeat from ★ 6 times **more**, then
repeat from † to † once, 5 dc in same sp as first dc, ch 1,
hdc in first dc to form last ch-3 sp: 224 sts and 48 sps.

Rnd 12: Ch 3, 4 dc in last ch-3 sp made, ch 1, tr in
next ch-1 sp, tr in next 5 tr and in next ch-1 sp, ch 1,
★ (5 dc, ch 3, 5 dc) in next ch-3 sp, ch 1, tr in next
ch-1 sp, tr in next 5 tr and in next ch-1 sp, ch 1; repeat
from ★ around, 5 dc in same sp as first dc, ch 1, hdc in
first dc to form last ch-3 sp: 272 sts and 48 sps.

Rnd 13: Ch 3, 4 dc in last ch-3 sp made, ch 1, tr in
next ch-1 sp, tr in next 7 tr and in next ch-1 sp, ch 1,
★ (5 dc, ch 3, 5 dc) in next ch-3 sp, ch 1, tr in next
ch-1 sp, tr in next 7 tr and in next ch-1 sp, ch 1; repeat
from ★ around, 5 dc in same sp as first dc, ch 1, hdc in
first dc to form last ch-3 sp: 304 sts and 48 sps.

Rnd 14: Ch 3, 4 dc in last ch-3 sp made, ch 1, skip
next 5 dc, tr in next 9 tr, ch 1, skip next ch-1 sp, ★ (5 dc,
ch 3, 5 dc) in next ch-3 sp, ch 1, skip next 5 dc, tr in
next 9 tr, ch 1, skip next ch-1 sp; repeat from ★ around,
5 dc in same sp as first dc, ch 1, hdc in first dc to form
last ch-3 sp; do **not** finish off.

Continued on page 53

51

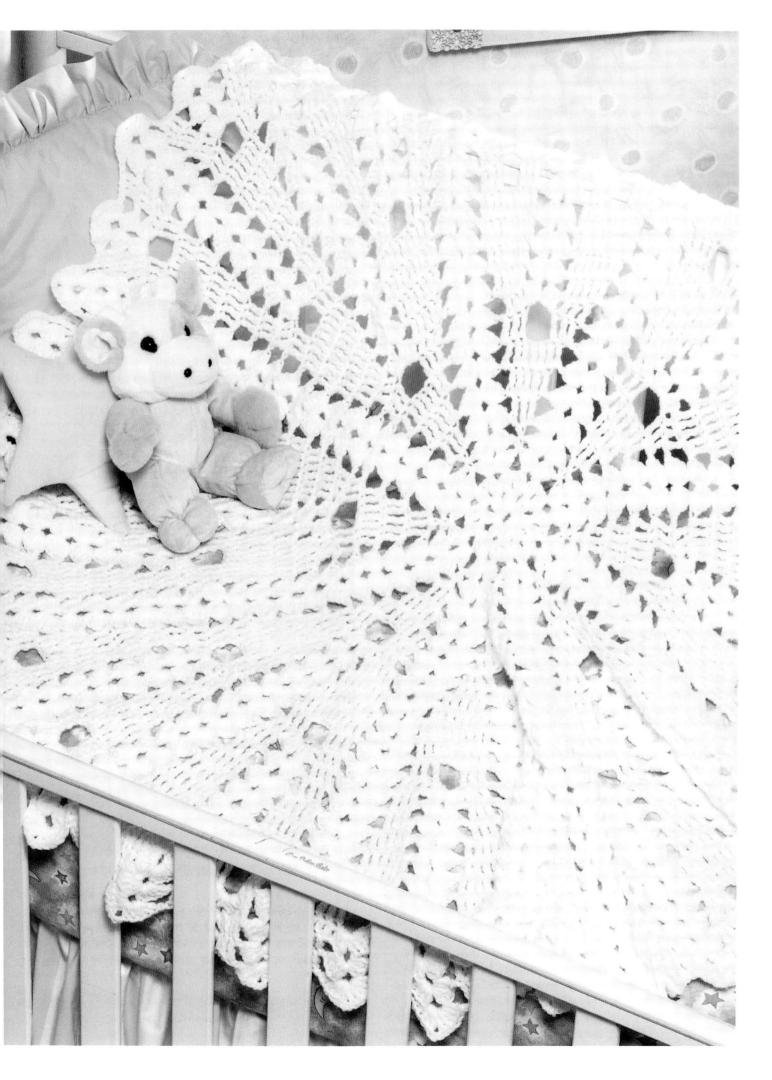

Rnd 15: Ch 3, 4 dc in last ch-3 sp made, ch 1, skip next 5 dc, tr in next 3 tr, ch 3, skip next 3 tr, tr in next 3 tr, ch 1, skip next ch-1 sp, ★ (5 dc, ch 3, 5 dc) in next ch-3 sp, ch 1, skip next 5 dc, tr in next 3 tr, ch 3, skip next 3 tr, tr in next 3 tr, ch 1, skip next ch-1 sp; repeat from ★ around, 5 dc in same sp as first dc, ch 1, hdc in first dc to form last ch-3 sp: 256 sts and 64 sps.

Rnd 16: Ch 3, 4 dc in last ch-3 sp made, ★ † ch 1, skip next 5 dc, tr in next tr, dc in next tr, hdc in next tr, ch 1, (3 dc, ch 3, 3 dc) in next ch-3 sp, ch 1, hdc in next tr, dc in next tr, tr in next tr, ch 1, skip next ch-1 sp †, (5 dc, ch 3, 5 dc) in next ch-3 sp; repeat from ★ 14 times **more**, then repeat from † to † once, 5 dc in same sp as first dc, ch 1, hdc in first dc to form last ch-3 sp: 352 sts and 96 sps.

Rnd 17: Ch 3, 4 dc in last ch-3 sp made, ★ † ch 1, skip next 5 dc and next ch-1 sp, tr in next 3 sts, ch 1, skip next ch-1 sp, (4 dc, ch 3, 4 dc) in next ch-3 sp, ch 1, skip next 3 dc and next ch-1 sp, tr in next 3 sts, ch 1, skip next ch-1 sp †, (5 dc, ch 3, 5 dc) in next ch-3 sp; repeat from ★ 14 times **more**, then repeat from † to † once, 5 dc in same sp as first dc, ch 1, hdc in first dc to form last ch-3 sp: 384 sts and 96 sps.

Rnd 18: Ch 3, 4 dc in last ch-3 sp made, ch 1, skip next ch-1 sp, tr in next 3 tr, ch 1, skip next ch-1 sp, ★ (5 dc, ch 3, 5 dc) in next ch-3 sp, ch 1, skip next ch-1 sp, tr in next 3 tr, ch 1, skip next ch-1 sp; repeat from ★ around, 5 dc in same sp as first dc, ch 1, hdc in first dc to form last ch-3 sp: 416 sts and 96 sps.

Rnd 19: Ch 3, 4 dc in last ch-3 sp made, ch 1, tr in next ch-1 sp, tr in next 3 tr and in next ch-1 sp, ch 1, ★ (5 dc, ch 3, 5 dc) in next ch-3 sp, ch 1, tr in next ch-1 sp, tr in next 3 tr and in next ch-1 sp, ch 1; repeat from ★ around, 5 dc in same sp as first dc, ch 1, hdc in first dc to form last ch-3 sp: 480 sts and 96 sps.

Rnds 20 and 21: Ch 3, 4 dc in last ch-3 sp made, ch 1, skip next 5 dc, tr in next 5 tr, ch 1, skip next ch-1 sp, ★ (5 dc, ch 3, 5 dc) in next ch-3 sp, ch 1, skip next 5 dc, tr in next 5 tr, ch 1, skip next ch-1 sp; repeat from ★ around, 5 dc in same sp as first dc, ch 1, hdc in first dc to form last ch-3 sp.

Rnd 22: Ch 3, 4 dc in last ch-3 sp made, ch 1, tr in next ch-1 sp, tr in next 5 tr and in next ch-1 sp, ch 1, ★ (5 dc, ch 3, 5 dc) in next ch-3 sp, ch 1, tr in next ch-1 sp, tr in next 5 tr and in next ch-1 sp, ch 1; repeat from ★ around, 5 dc in same sp as first dc, ch 1, hdc in first dc to form last ch-3 sp: 544 sts and 96 sps.

Rnd 23: Ch 3, 4 dc in last ch-3 sp made, ch 1, skip next 5 dc, tr in next 7 tr, ch 1, skip next ch-1 sp, ★ (5 dc ch 3, 5 dc) in next ch-3 sp, ch 1, skip next 5 dc, tr in next 7 tr, ch 1, skip next ch-1 sp; repeat from ★ around, 5 dc in same sp as first dc, ch 1, hdc in first dc to form last ch-3 sp.

Rnd 24: Ch 3, 4 dc in last ch-3 sp made, ch 1, tr in next ch-1 sp and in next 2 tr, ch 3, skip next 3 tr, tr in next 2 tr and in next ch-1 sp, ch 1, ★ (5 dc, ch 3, 5 dc) in next ch-3 sp, ch 1, tr in next ch-1 sp and in next 2 tr, ch 3, skip next 3 tr, tr in next 2 tr and in next ch-1 sp, ch 1; repeat from ★ around, 5 dc in same sp as first dc, ch 1, hdc in first dc to form last ch-3 sp: 512 sts and 128 sps.

Rnd 25: Ch 3, 4 dc in last ch-3 sp made, ★ † ch 1, skip next 5 dc, tr in next tr, dc in next tr, hdc in next tr, ch 1, (3 dc, ch 3, 3 dc) in next ch-3 sp, ch 1, hdc in next tr, dc in next tr, tr in next tr, ch 1, skip next ch-1 sp †, (5 dc, ch 3, 5 dc) in next ch-3 sp; repeat from ★ 30 times **more**, then repeat from † to † once, 5 dc in same sp as first dc, ch 1, hdc in first dc to form last ch-3 sp: 704 sts and 192 sps.

Rnd 26: Ch 3, 4 dc in last ch-3 sp made, ★ † ch 1, skip next 5 dc and next ch-1 sp, tr in next 3 sts, ch 1, skip next ch-1 sp, (4 dc, ch 3, 4 dc) in next ch-3 sp, ch 1, skip next 3 dc and next ch-1 sp, tr in next 3 sts, ch 1, skip next ch-1 sp †, (5 dc, ch 3, 5 dc) in next ch-3 sp; repeat from ★ 30 times **more**, then repeat from † to † once, 5 dc in same sp as first dc, dc in first dc to form last ch-3 sp: 768 sts and 192 sps.

Rnd 27: Ch 3, (4 dc, ch 3, 5 dc) in last ch-3 sp made, ch 1, skip next 5 dc, tr in next 3 tr, ch 1, skip next ch-1 sp, ★ (5 dc, ch 3, 5 dc) in next ch-3 sp, ch 1, skip next 5 dc, tr in next 3 tr, ch 1, skip next ch-1 sp; repeat from ★ around; join with slip st to first dc, finish off.

Design by Sarah Anne Phillips.